Welcome to the Sequel

to

I Wish I Could Say I Was Sorry

US Amazon Top 100 Title*

#1 TRAVEL
#1 TRAVEL BIOGRAPHY
#4 MEMOIR
#5 NONFICTION

250 US REVIEWS
Av 4.00 STARS
55 UK REVIEWS
Av 4.7 STARS

I Wish I Could Say
I Was Sorry...

SUSIE KELLY

*#35 Paid Chart Jan 2014

'*A Child Called It* meets *Out Of Africa* in this stunning memoir of a woman's 1950s childhood in Kenya. Filled with candid humor and insights, this authentic tale captures one woman's incredible coming-of-age journey.' BookBub

"What an astounding story, sometimes true life experiences are better than fiction."

"Heartbreakingly real."

"This memoir kept me up. I could not stop reading this. An almost idyllic early girlhood that becomes more and more dysfunctional. What a story!"

"Best book I have read in years."

"The whole story is a great tug on the heart strings. I couldn't put the book down and have every intention of reading it again."

"Spellbinding."

"A dysfunctional families true story that had me shedding real tears in some places and laughing out loud in other places as I read. A marvellous book."

"I am blown away by such talent."

SAFARI ANTS, BAGGY PANTS AND ELEPHANTS

A Kenyan Odyssey

Susie Kelly

blackbird

Copyright © Susie Kelly 2017

Published by Blackbird Digital Books
www.blackbird-books.com

A CIP catalogue record for this book is available from the British Library
ISBN 9780995473577

The moral right of the author has been asserted.
Cover design by First Impressions Inc
Dreamstime Cover Image © Niserin | Mount Kilimanjaro. Savanna In
Amboseli, Kenya Photo
Illustrated Photographs © Susie Kelly

To all those who love and care for all the creatures of our world, from the smallest to the largest

CONTENTS

Chapter One

SPEAK SWAHILI: JAMBO – HELLO

2014 was an uneventful year for us until November, when two things happened almost simultaneously.

The first thing that happened was that I was invited to the nearby town of Charroux to meet two ladies who were organising a literary festival to be held the following year. We chatted over delicate French patisserie and fancy pots of tea that were served accompanied by egg-timers to ensure optimum brewing time, and an hour later I had accepted their proposal that I should become the patron of the Charroux Literary Festival. It was rather exciting, as I had never previously been a patron of anything, and I was delighted to be involved in bringing the literary spotlight to this quaint historic, little town.

The second thing that happened was the following morning when I received an email from my longest-standing friend, Vivien, owner of *As You Like It Safaris* in Kenya. It read:

'You and Terry are coming on a safari next year. I am sending a copy of your itinerary in a separate email.'

My immediate reaction was that she was joking, that it was some kind of meme where you send friends a spoof email. I sent a smiley icon in reply.

Later that day, the itinerary arrived. It covered seventeen days, including stays in five of Kenya's greatest wildlife reserves and two of its most exclusive clubs. We would be travelling with members of the *95th Bomb Group Memorial Foundation*, people who keep alive and honour those who served and fell in the air campaign over central Europe during WWII.

It sounded idyllic but was completely out of the question, not least because it conflicted with the literary festival dates.

Over the next month, I wrote explaining all the reasons we would not be able to go, which Vivien airily brushed aside as mere excuses, including my commitment to the festival.

'They will manage perfectly well without you,' she declared. "You're only the patron, not a guest speaker or organiser.' That put me in my place.

Terry shared my reaction that we couldn't go. There was the expense, the question of having our animals cared for, the fact that our property was for sale and the idea of flying thousands of miles to do something we had never considered doing.

But like a dripping tap Vivien kept chipping away, brushing aside all our ifs and buts. She is and has always been the most positive person I know. There is nothing that cannot be accomplished if you put your mind to it.

The organisers of the literary festival were insistent that we should not miss an opportunity that would probably never come our way again, thus proving Vivien's point. :)

By January, we were beginning to weaken and by March I'd booked our flights.

Chapter Two

SPEAK SWAHILI: HABARI? – HOW ARE YOU?

Once we had decided to go, everything ran like clockwork with a few clicks of a mouse.

Online application for our Kenya visas was quick and easy, and they were available to download twelve hours later.

Through *Trusted Housesitters*, I found a couple who would come to look after our animals – two dogs, one parrot and two pygmy goats – while we were away.

I was able to organise travel and health insurance, book our flights, train tickets and buy our luggage without moving from my desk.

How did people manage before the advent of mobile phones, internet and email? Imagine those early long safaris with porters carrying fridges, sofas and cocktail cabinets, tents and collapsible baths, crates of gin and cooking utensils. Imagine the logistics of things even as simple as organising when and where to meet, and how to get in touch if anything didn't go according to schedule, when the only means of communication were handwritten letters or telegrams.

It was surprising how quickly time shot by. When we'd first begun talking about the trip, it had been nine months away. Now the days flew past, and I began to get unspeakably anxious that something would go wrong, because I had come to realise how very much I wanted to get back to the country where I had lived for nearly twenty years and enjoyed some of the very best days of my life. When I had left more than forty years ago, it was due to personal circumstances, and even after living in France for over twenty years, in my heart Kenya will always be 'home'.

Our housesitters arrived several weeks before our departure to give us all time to make sure that the arrangement would suit everybody, including the dogs whose welfare is always our principle concern, especially as Tally was 14 years old.

I made lists and more lists of what we needed to take with us, trying to keep everything to a minimum as I've always been a 'travel light' person, happy with a couple of pairs of jeans and a few tops, sufficient underwear and something to read. However I hadn't been very well for the last year, and the medication I was taking caused my weight to fluctuate rather dramatically. I never knew what size I'd wake up from one day to the next, and rather than pack too many clothes or garments that may be too small, I opted for clothes that may be too large.

We had been asked to take gifts for Kenyan children, and had stocked up with clothing, games and educational material. By the time we had added hygiene products, a hair dryer, a laptop, our Kindles, notebooks and mobile phones, we each had a bulging suitcase and a full backpack that left no room for our cameras. I had only recently taken an interest in photography but was not at all relishing the prospect of lugging around a DSLR that was as big as and weighed as much as a house brick, nor a lens as long as my arm and weighing as much as a breeze block, so I had bought an Olympus mirrorless OMD camera small enough to fit in a pocket, together with a lightweight zoom lens able to deliver stunning photos. Terry had been so impressed that he had also abandoned his house brick and bought an identical camera to mine.

Three days before our departure, we were thrown into

panic when one of our housesitters was unwell and announced that they might have to leave. I started frantically searching *Trusted Housesitters* for a replacement, and whisked the patient off to our doctor, who immediately sent us to a specialist. We are so very lucky with the French health system. There is no hanging around waiting for an appointment. It took half a day of my time that was needed elsewhere to finalise our arrangements, and pumped my blood pressure up to its limit, but the specialist found nothing more serious than dehydration and told the patient to drink more water.

Why I worked myself up so much about the packing I have no idea, but I emptied, rearranged and repacked everything at least twice daily in the final days before we left. On the morning of departure, I meticulously re-packed yet again, ticked off every item on my lists, zipping up the bags, confident that we had everything we needed. Terry loaded them into the boot of Mike and Jenny's car, our kind friends who had volunteered to drive us to the station to catch our train to Paris.

Chapter Three

SPEAK SWAHILI: ASANTE – THANK YOU

At the station, I dug around in my backpack for my make-up bag before I remembered that I'd put it in the suitcase, which I proceeded to unpack onto the chairs in the station waiting room. Worryingly, the make-up bag was not there, so I began a more thorough search of the backpack. After I'd emptied that as well – people were now staring as piles of clothes were building up on the seats – it wasn't there either. Then I recalled that just before we left I'd touched up my mascara, and I could clearly visualise the bag sitting on the side of the basin in our bathroom at home. So much for all that careful packing. Now I had no make-up, but that shouldn't be a problem; there'd be an opportunity to buy some at the airport. Then my heart lurched. Where was my essential medication? I broke out in a sweat as I recalled putting all the tablets and capsules into the make-up bag.

There was no time to go home, and no way to buy any more without a prescription. I'd probably die. Well, not really. That was me being a drama queen. I could possibly survive without them for three weeks; or maybe not. There are certain drugs that I have to take daily in order to keep ticking over smoothly.

I shoved all the stuff back into the bags and dug around in the pocket of my backpack for my Kindle. When the world is falling down around your ears, the only sensible thing you can do is either sleep or read. My fingers connected with something that rustled. There were the strips of tablets. Yes! I'd saved my own life.

The TGV train ride up to Paris was comfortable and

uneventful. Our Spanish friend, Miguel, was living near Paris so we had arranged to meet him at the airport and spend a few hours together, leaving plenty of time to catch our flight. From the platform, I spotted him standing, waving from the first floor. Terry piled our bags onto a trolley and headed for the lift, telling me to go ahead and wait with Miguel, which I did.

We waited and waited, looking expectantly each time the lift door opened. Time after time it disgorged travellers and trolleys, but it did not disgorge Terry. We looked down onto the platform and saw him still queuing. There was only one working lift, and it was very small. We waited some more.

Finally the last passengers arrived and the lift was empty, and so was the platform. There was no sign of Terry.

We wandered around to see if we had somehow missed him, but after scouring the whole of the first floor he was nowhere to be seen.

It was more than 20 minutes since we had arrived and I was once again in panic mode. Had he changed his mind, stepped back onto the train with our luggage? Had he been taken ill and carted away? Kidnapped? How could he have vanished just like that? I was considering sending out a message over the announcement system, although whether anything could be heard over the rattling trolleys, rumbling suitcase wheels, shouted telephone conversations, general buzz and confusion seemed doubtful, when Miguel took my arm and pointed to Terry another level up, standing, looking irritated.

'Where on earth have you been?' he asked, taking the words out my mouth. After a brief exchange that was a mixture of exasperation and relief, he explained that he had pushed the lift button indicating 'Departures'. Logical, but wrong, because we were waiting on the first floor, and Departures is on the second floor. It was the first indication that navigation at Charles de Gaulle airport was not entirely straightforward. At least we were now all together and I suggested we looked for somewhere to have a drink. I felt in need of a nice gin and tonic, and something to eat. No, said Miguel, we needed to go to Terminal 1.

But surely we were already in Terminal 1, I asked. No, he replied, this is the train terminal. We need to get to the plane terminal. We looked in vain for directions, but the sixth person I spoke to pointed us to the shuttle that would take us there. Without Miguel, I thought to myself, that we would have sat for hours in blissful ignorance at the train terminal and missed our flight. For anybody using this airport for the first time, I recommend giving yourself far more time than you think you need.

This is just my opinion, and others may disagree, but I found Charles de Gaulle airport quite hideous and extraordinarily passenger-hostile. I'd travelled through many airports in my life, but never one as disorganised as this. Maybe I was out of practice, but really, it seemed so difficult to find your way around this place. I'm not the only one.

In November 15, 2011, Karrie Jacobs who writes on urban architecture for http://www.travelandleisure.com, described the airport thus:

'It's not simply non-linear, but anti-linear to the point where no one – least of all passengers – ever knows quite what to expect. In part this is because, unlike most of the world's major airports, it reflects the vision of a single individual, former Chief Architect of the Aéroports de Paris, Paul Andreu. Now 73, he began work on Terminal 1 at 29. It is very much a young man's idea of things to come. The main 11-story building is round, constructed from that rugged poured concrete that architects so loved back then, with a doughnut hole at the center.'

I could not argue with that. It's bleak, colourless, unwelcoming, and we couldn't find anywhere pleasant for a light meal. Like us, Miguel is vegetarian, and we ended up buying weak coffee and sad pieces of cake from a snack bar where the only alternative was cheese and ham baguette. However, at least we were in good company and enjoying a couple of hours together while I secretly geared myself up for the next panic attack. I had started shaking from a combination of excitement and anxiety, because I had doubts that we would actually be getting on the flight. I'd booked online through Expedia at an extraordinary discount – less than one-third of the usual price at that time of year – and all I had was an email confirmation and a debit on our bank account. Expedia's assurance that the email confirmation was all that was necessary had not entirely convinced me, and I had opened the printed email so many times to read it that by the time we arrived at the Swiss International Air check-in desk, it was starting to fall apart.

I handed the crumpled paper across the counter waiting for the puzzled look that it would surely elicit, signalling that I'd been a complete idiot to have been taken in.

The check-in lady squashed it flat and ironed it out with her hand, a slight frown on her brow as she began typing into her computer. Unsmiling, she looked up and asked for our passports. Checking to see if we were on the 'Wanted' list, I thought gloomily.

She burrowed around in a drawer for a few moments, tapped into her computer again, and then handed back our passports, together with our tickets and a brilliant red-lipstick smile.

'Thank you. You may go through to the departure lounge now. Enjoy your flight with Swiss International Air.'

Our suitcases glided out of sight. Hopefully they would reach Nairobi at the same time as we did.

I switched off panic mode. We were on our way.

Chapter Four

SPEAK SWAHILI: PESI PESI – QUICKLY

The departure lounge was more hospitable than the terminal and the coffee was good. I had a look in the Duty Free shops for some replacement make-up, but there was a very poor selection and what there was, was all far more than I would normally spend.

Although the first stage of our journey was just a quick hop to Zurich, we were served drinks, a snack and several goodies including exquisite Swiss chocolate. I thought we were going to enjoy flying Swiss International.

Zurich airport is everything that Charles de Gaulle isn't. It's modern, sparkling, welcoming, comfortable, organised and the coffee is good. The staff are courteous, helpful and all speak English; there is a wide choice of good places to eat and spacious wash rooms. It's a monument to consumerism. Polished shop windows of boutiques selling the world's most luxurious caviare, chocolate, watches, leather goods, jewellery, electric bicycles, wines, spirits and champagne are reflected on the shiny mirror-bright floor. There's not a fingerprint to be seen.

It epitomised my idea of Swiss efficiency and enterprise. Amongst these palaces of plenty, I was pleased to find a tinted moisturiser and a lipstick at the kind of price I habitually pay, which is less than 20 euros. It wasn't much, but it was better than having no make-up at all for the next three weeks.

The only downside of our cheap tickets was a 10-hour overnight layover in Zurich. As our luggage was somewhere between Paris and Nairobi with all our clothes and hygiene supplies, we decided that we would sleep as best we could in the airport lounge.

As best we could wasn't that good. We traipsed from one floor to another, seeking out a corner to ourselves. When we found the perfect place, horror of horrors – there was a roaring snorer nearby, and even with my earplugs jammed as hard as they would go, I could still hear him. We kept trundling around until we found an unpopulated, quiet and relatively dark corner, where we tried to lie down across the rigid plastic chairs with the slightly up-tilted sides that stick into your person no matter how you twist and turn, thoughtfully designed to prevent people lying down on them. Terry managed to snooze with his jacket wrapped around his head, and I had very nearly dropped off, when suddenly there was a noise like the rumbling of thunder or a volcanic eruption, accompanied by squeals and loud voices, then the place was flooded with light. For a moment I thought a bomb had gone off, but it seemed we had chosen to sleep next to one of the ports, and a plane load of disembarking passengers streamed past, trotting and chattering, heels clattering and suitcase wheels rattling. By the time they had all dispersed and darkness had been restored, I was wide awake and remained so for the rest of the night.

In my backpack were two items I never travel without – an ample supply of food and my Kindle. Whatever happens, with something to read and something to eat, I'm happy. Unable to get back to sleep, I consoled myself with two cheese and onion sandwiches, and the knowledge that with an 8-hour flight ahead of us there would be plenty of time to catch up on our sleep then.

Daylight arrived beneath a thick grey layer of fog and an announcement that our flight would be delayed for two hours. We freshened up and found an excellent breakfast, then made our way to the departure lounge, where we drank coffee and read our Kindles. The flight was fully booked and we had the novel experience of being an ethnic minority – the only two white faces among our fellow passengers.

It had been decades since I'd last flown long-haul. Over the previous 20 years, my flying had all been cattle-class between France and the UK. I'd forgotten how enjoyable flying could be in a comfortable aircraft with an attentive cabin crew constantly circulating with drinks, magazines and snacks. Lunch was served early to give passengers the opportunity to sleep away the long flight. When booking, I'd requested vegetarian meals and had been offered a choice of vegan, Western vegetarian, Chinese vegetarian, Hindu vegetarian or Jain vegetarian. I'd opted for the Hindu, and our meal was an excellent curry that could compare favourably with any one might have in a good restaurant.

I was too excited to be tired despite having been awake for 32 hours, and although there was a wide choice of music and films, instead I watched the flight's path on the television, millimetre by millimetre as it crossed Europe, the Mediterranean and the desert landscapes of Libya, Egypt and Sudan.

The date was 20th August, 2015. As the plane swallowed up the miles, I remembered my first journey to Kenya which had begun 61 years ago, almost to the day, on 26th August 1954.

Chapter Five

SPEAK SWAHILI: POLE POLE – SLOWLY

My father, a commercial accountant, had been asked by his firm to move to Kenya. It was an opportunity to be taken with both hands, a chance to escape from battered, bruised London to a new life in a new country. It was our good fortune that in the 1950s air travel was the more expensive option, and so my father's employers paid for our passages by sea, which gave us three weeks aboard the S.S. Kenya Castle, an elegant ship painted in the lavender livery of the *Union Castle* line that sailed weekly from England to Africa.

What an adventure that was for a kid who had never been outside austere post-war Britain. We were a middle-class family and lived comfortably by the standards of that era, but I could not have imagined the life we were leading at sea. Every day was a holiday, with the scenery constantly changing, film shows, fancy dress parties and games on deck. Adults dressed for dinner and danced to a live orchestra. I think until then the most exotic fruit I had eaten was an occasional banana or a tangerine at Christmas, and now there was fresh pineapple, mangoes and pawpaws (which Americans call papaya). You could eat as much as you liked, and there was cake for tea every day, not just on Sunday. Each morning, stewards served cups of hot Bovril when we were still in chilly Atlantic waters, and once we were in the Mediterranean, ice cream as the days grew warmer. There was the excitement of sailing into ports for trips ashore, and cheap shopping in Aden, where my father bought an anniversary clock in a glass case, which was destined to stand on the mantelpiece of our new home. Of all the things I remembered about that voyage, it was the sight of camel trains silhouetted against the sunset, swaying along the banks of the Suez Canal that I remember most vividly.

In the baking temperature of the Red Sea, I was covered in prickly heat rash, and kept having nosebleeds for no reason, but it did nothing to spoil the wonderment of our journey, and was a negligible price to pay for never again having to wear a liberty bodice, thick woolly stockings and a red knitted pixie hat.

When we docked at Mombasa, we followed the stream of passengers bouncing down the gangway to the docks into the blinding sunshine. The heat ricocheted off the tarmac and buildings, hitting us like a wave. The noise was intense – shouts, songs, snapping ships' chains – and the smells were of hot engines, spices and human sweat. The scenery was a kaleidoscope of colour – the bluest ocean, the shining green of coconut palms and wide-leafed banana trees, the glistening brown bodies, barefoot, wearing ragged shorts or colourful cotton *kikois* around their hips, carrying loads on their heads or pushing them in wooden handcarts.

Mummy and I stood in the hot Customs shed holding hands, while my father dealt with the immigration formalities. I had not expected Africa to be like this, with all these white people, neat buildings and motor vehicles. Where was the jungle, the monkeys and parrots, the elephants?

With several hours to wait before our onward journey to Nairobi, we went with some people my parents had made friends with to have lunch at a hotel, and I still remember our meal that seemed so sophisticated, so foreign – chicken in the basket served with pineapple fritters.

In the late afternoon, we climbed onto the train that would tug its way through the night up to Nairobi, 300 miles away, and the magic began.

From the window of our sleeper, I gazed out at the

landscape that was flat and verdant, with thatched round huts among groves of banana plants and coconut palms. Little children stood smiling and waving at the train as it passed. Although I looked hard I couldn't see any elephants, but overall my impression of Africa was improving.

Darkness fell very quickly. A man walked along the corridor of the train sounding a gong to announce that dinner was served. It's funny how when I look back now so many of my memories are related to food. Maybe it was something to do with being a post-war baby in the years when food rationing was still in force.

Each dining table was laid with starched bright white tablecloths, polished silver cutlery, a small vase of flowers and a neat little lamp. Our waiter was the first African man I had been really close to, and I was surprised that he was not wearing a leopard skin, but an ankle-length loose white garment – a *kanzu* – a red fez and white gloves.

By the time we returned to our cabin the seats had been made up into bunks, with crisp sheets and rough green blankets to ward off the chilly night air. We settled down to sleep as the train crept upwards through the night, and through the Tsavo area where a couple of lions had terrorised and eaten a number of the men working to build this railway at the end of the 19th century.

I woke when a crack of light appeared at the side of the blind over the window, and I peered out onto the Athi plains in the morning sun. The green of the coastal region had been replaced by golden grasses where tens of thousands of wild animals grazed. Giraffe, zebra, antelope and gazelles, stumpy-legged warthogs with curved tusks and tails like antennae sticking straight up. Ostriches, storks, vultures. A teeming mass of striped, patterned, plump creatures munching their way across the plains... Still no elephants, though.

An hour later and three weeks after we had left London,

the train pulled in to the railway station in Nairobi, noisy and colourful, smelly and vibrant. We were met by one of my father's new colleagues, who drove us up the dual carriageway – then the Princess Elizabeth Highway – lined with bougainvillea in colours ranging from white through pale orange to brilliant vermilion, to our hotel standing in green lawns. Frangipani trees sprayed the air with their sweet, rich smell, and lizards chased over the paving stones.

Even without the elephants, I fell in love with Kenya. I had fallen in love then, and that love had never faded. It has always been there.

Chapter Six

SPEAK SWAHILI: NZURI – GOOD

Back from my reverie, on board the plane, the flight tracker showed that we were clipping the corner of Ethiopia. Night was beginning to fall as we crossed into Kenya, and the airport was just a few minutes away.

I thought back to every other flight I've made in and out of Nairobi. First, from the old RAF station at Eastleigh in 1957, when I was sent back to boarding school. Then in 1963 from the new Embakasi airport, back to England to visit the mother I hadn't seen for 7 years, returning a month later to an airport teeming with screaming, waving teenage girls because Cliff Richard and the Shadows were on the same flight. In 1968, recently married, I'd flown to England and Italy to visit family. Four years later, I'd flown away with a broken heart at leaving Kenya to start a new life in England. The last time I'd been back was in 1976 to collect my two children whom my husband had kidnapped. At that time, Embakasi was still a neat and informal small airport where you stepped off the aircraft and a 20-second walk took you straight into the terminal.

Looking down onto Jomo Kenyatta International Airport prior to landing was like looking down onto a space station, the lights of the city stretching into infinity. I had of course realised that after 40 years things would have changed dramatically, yet I was still surprised by the size of the airport named after Jomo Kenyatta, a remarkable man, accused and found guilty of masterminding the Mau Mau freedom fighter movement and imprisoned by us (the British) in harsh conditions for 7 years. As the date for his release approached, Europeans had feared reprisals, and many left Kenya. However, he had shown no resentment for his mistreatment, and called for '*Harambee*' – let's work together. In 1964, Mzee – as he was affectionately known – it means 'old man' – became the first President of the Republic of Kenya and steered Kenya into a stable, prosperous new country.

The wheels touched the tarmac, the brakes came on, we were thrust forward and then pushed back into our seats, and rolled to a halt.

I've never really felt 'English' and I'll never be truly 'French'. Having spent my formative years in Kenya, it is the country where I lived many of my happiest moments, and some of my worst. So many memories, so many ghosts. Although we were tourists, I still felt in my heart that I was returning 'home'. Unexpectedly, my eyes filled with tears and I was overcome with emotion. When the doors opened and we climbed down the stairs, I had a Pope John Paul II moment and felt like kneeling down to kiss the tarmac. For Terry, on his first visit to Africa, I thought it must feel very foreign, very strange being a white man surrounded by Africans but it felt just right to me.

The night air fell upon us in the old familiar way, like a soft silken shawl.

A shuttle bus with merry African music playing had replaced the 20-second walk to the terminal. Two years previously, a fire at the airport had completely destroyed the Arrivals hall, and while that was being rebuilt it was housed temporarily on the ground floor of the multi-storey car park. All things considered it was well-organised. Security was tight; unsmiling but polite. Our luggage took no longer to arrive than it does at any airport. I noticed that many of our fellow passengers had swaddled their cases tightly in layers of that very strong plastic wrapping used to protect furniture during removals to safeguard their luggage from knocks, bumps, tears and interference during baggage handling.

With our flight having been delayed by two hours, as we pushed our trolleys out into the front of the building I wondered if there would actually be anybody waiting there to meet us. We stared into the waiting crowd until I saw the *As You Like It Safaris* sign, and the smiling faces and outstretched hands of two of the guides who would be responsible for our enjoyment and safety for the next 17 days. They introduced themselves: Steve would drive us to our hotel – but Kamara had another three-hour wait for some more members of our party.

The traffic around the airport was just short of pandemonium. Where once there would have been a dozen cars angle-parked outside the terminal building, there was now a dual carriageway crowded with arriving passengers, departing passengers, people waiting for or delivering them, hooting cars, taxis, policeman swinging batons and security barriers leading in and out of the complex. Steve predicted that it could take up to two and a half hours to reach our hotel in Nairobi, a distance of 10 miles that used to be an easy, twenty-minute journey with little traffic on the road. There were hundreds of vehicles nose-to-tail, and what used to be vacant land was covered with modern buildings. On the edges of the road, cattle and goats grazed within millimetres of the passing traffic, and ramshackle stalls offered wares from clothing to vegetables, mobile phones and snacks. Beneath the street lamps, crowds of people milled around, the air noisy with laughter, music and chatter.

Steve weaved the Land Cruiser through the traffic with the nonchalance of somebody used to driving where nobody allowed the rules of the road to impede their journey, neatly avoiding suicidal chickens and a herd of goats that trotted across the road a few feet ahead of us. He handed each of us our personal *As You Like It Safaris* welcome packs, containing a laminated itinerary of our movements over the next 17 days, profiles of our guides, fellow travellers and support staff, a notebook and pen, a booklet listing all the birds and mammals we were likely to see and could tick off, and a gorgeous Kenyan *kikoi*. With one of these versatile colourful cotton rectangles, you are ready for anything as they can be used as articles of clothing, baby-carriers, headgear, beach mats, shopping bags, towels, curtains, sheets, table cloths, picnic rugs and any other purpose that you can think of for a rectangle of strong cotton.

Thanks to Steve's driving and the traffic flowing well, we reached the Nairobi Serena hotel quickly. The doorman, resplendent in a cream long-coated suit, brocade waistcoat and peaked cap, greeted us like royalty while porters unloaded our bags. Kenyans are naturally warm and smiling people, and when it comes to giving service they excel and take pride in doing their utmost to please you wholeheartedly, which I guess is one of the reasons so many people love this country. From the hotel gardens, the old familiar night sounds of the frogs' chorus and crickets stirred the darkness.

As our bags vanished into the lift, the receptionist said she had been asked to signal our arrival, and a member of staff led us through the hotel towards the dining room.

When it comes to decor I love warmth, comfort, and understated luxury, which is what the hotel offered. An elegant, harmonious blend of European, Arabic and East African architecture and art, with oriental rugs in deep, rich colours lying on the polished wooden floors, gleaming brassware, carved wood and ethnic sculptures. Warm, subtle lighting created an atmosphere of hospitality and comfort, the furniture beckoning us to sit down, make ourselves comfortable, feel at home. I've never liked chandeliers, ornate mirrors, gilt picture frames and rigidly-upholstered furniture. Balmy air drifted in from the gardens through the open doors.

I heard rapid footsteps and turned to see the person who was responsible for our being there. My friend for over 50 years from the time we met as pony-mad teenagers, Vivien. She is lean and brown and tiny, with black wavy hair, bright blue eyes and a glorious smile. She has more energy and determination than anybody I've ever met. For years she had been telling me we must go on safari with her. 'You need to do this, Susan.' 'You mustn't leave it too long,' 'Live for the day!' 'Stop making excuses!' 'What are you waiting for!' 'Susan, yesterday is gone, tomorrow may never happen! You have to act now!' 'If you don't do this, Susan, you'll regret it for the rest of your life.' I don't know why she always calls me Susan; she's the only person who does so, and although I associate it with school and being told off, we've been friends for too long to let a little thing like a name stand between us.

As a child, I changed schools frequently and lost contact with school friends, as I did with most of my adult friends when I left Kenya. All except for Vivien. Our friendship has spanned the decades, the oceans and the continents, and is as strong as ever, and I am honoured to be her friend. Although our lives diverged and we both moved around the world, and despite losing touch for long periods, we had always managed to find each other again one way or another.

The first time we met, I was riding my adored pony, Cinderella, in a field close to the stables where I kept her a few miles outside of Nairobi. I noticed somebody standing watching me, and rode over to her. 'What a beautiful pony,' she said. I have to tell you that I was very possessive of Cinderella and had never considered letting anybody else ride her, and I was also very much a loner who found it difficult to reach out to other people. There was something about this girl with the soft voice and big smile, and I surprised myself by dismounting and handing her the reins.

'Have a ride,' I said.

Through all the years, although usually separated by continents, our friendship has endured. It blossomed when she began to ride Cinderella at shows – she was a far superior horsewoman to me and if she suffered from nerves, she never showed it. I recognised that while I was content to be mediocre, she was somebody who was driven to excel at everything she did, and will always give her wholehearted best. For all the successes she has notched up, she remains unfailingly modest and self-deprecating.

'You made it!' she cried as we hugged and squealed like schoolgirls. She didn't look a day older than when we had last met eleven years previously, when she had come to France to house/pet sit for us when we toured around France in the collapsing campervan.

'Come and meet everyone,' she said, leading us into the dining room that opened out onto the floodlit gardens and swimming pool. The buffet offered every kind of salad, soup, vegetable, cooked meats and fish; there was a section where the chef would prepare a fresh stir fry, or grill; breads of every description, cheeses, fresh and cooked fruit, hot and cold desserts. The aroma was tantalising. How to choose from such a selection! Oh dear, there I go again. Food.

Most of our fellow guests had arrived earlier. They'd all travelled from the United States, entailing far longer journeys than ours, had finished eating, looked tired and ready to retire. It wasn't the time for in-depth introductions and lengthy conversations, which was a relief. While Terry is naturally gregarious and instantly at ease with new people, I find it rather an ordeal and need time to relax and come out from my shell. A delicious contentment and tiredness began to creep over me once we had eaten and enjoyed a glass of wine. I was looking forward to bed and a long lie-in next morning. Maybe we'd even take breakfast in bed, and start the day with a swim in the pool.

Vivien tapped her glass. 'We leave at 6.30am sharp

tomorrow,' she announced. 'So have your bags outside your room for collection and be down for breakfast by 6.00am.'

I gave an involuntary squeal of dismay, managing to disguise it with a cough. I'm not a morning person, more owl than lark. 6.30am Kenya time is 5.30am in France, where my normal getting-up time is about 8.30am.

Kenyans have their own way of telling the time. Sitting on the equator, Kenya's day and night are two equal periods of twelve hours. Sunrise begins at what in Western time is known as 7.00am, but which Kenyans refer to as hour one of the day – 'saa moja asubuhi'. Night falls at 7.00pm in Western time, which is 'saa moja usiku', hour one of the night. It is then repeated through the night, until the following morning arrives. Please learn these facts as I'll be testing you on them later.

A glass bowl of fragrant fresh roses stood on the writing desk in our elegant, spacious room, and the huge bed beckoned. My eyes were burning and I had the beginning of a tiredness headache, but even with the threat of the '12th hour of the night' getting-up time hanging over us, after Terry had turned off the lights I drew back the curtains and stood by the window for long while, looking out at the silhouettes of high-rise buildings, construction cranes and blinking telecommunication masts on Nairobi's nearby skyline.

Chapter Seven

SPEAK SWAHILI: SAWA SAWA – OK

There was an irritating, persistent buzzing noise somewhere. I dragged the pillow over my head and burrowed beneath the covers. The bed rebounded as Terry leapt up and started bouncing around the room. The buzzing noise came from the phone beside the bed. 'Good morning, Madame. It is 5.30,' said a bright and cheerful voice.

By the time I had groped my way awake, Terry was shaved and dressed and keen to go down for breakfast.

After a shower, I rummaged in my bag for some clean clothes. That was when I discovered that despite all my careful packing, repacking and re-repacking, I had failed to pack that essential item of underwear – a bra. Any bra. I had dressed for travel comfort because of our long journey, and had been wearing a soft stretchy camisole. I turned my bag inside out and upside down and searched every pocket, then I did the same to the backpack, but the brutal truth was that for the duration of our trip, I would be without a bra. The two soft stretchy camisoles would have to be my sole means of support for the next 17 days, and they were really not man enough for the job.

The only place I could buy any underwear is in Nairobi town, and we won't be going there. We don't have time. We are travelling as a group, not as individuals, and we leave at 6.30am.

When I wrote my first book about hiking across France, ill-equipped and under-funded, some readers left comments such as: 'Why didn't she just get on a train or take a taxi?' 'Why didn't she go and buy a new pair of boots/tent?'

My reaction was to smile wryly, realising that I had entirely failed to portray the absence of towns of any size in rural central France, and the non-existent public transport network. It can be 50 miles or more from even one small town to the next. There are no trains, buses or taxis between them, nor sports shops except in major cities. If you are hiking through the mountains you really do just have to get on with what you've got. Central France is hundreds of miles and a world away from Paris.

So that I don't make the same mistake again and for the benefit of readers who have not visited Kenya, I'll try to draw a picture. Nairobi is the capital and largest city in Kenya. It is a modern sophisticated city and there are definitely shops selling underwear. However, they would not be open at 6.00am, and we were not travelling independently, but as part of a group of 16 people leaving at daybreak for a 100-mile drive to our first destination, Amboseli. We would not pass any town of any size likely to sell ladies' lingerie. The same will apply to all our journeys. Even in larger towns, the likelihood of finding a lingerie shop really is about the same as winning the lottery, and if there was we would not be stopping there because our schedule was precise in order to give maximum value to all those in our group, who have come to see wild animals in their beautiful natural habitat; they would not be pleased to sit for several hours in a vehicle in the heat, in a chaotic town while I tried to find something to fit. So I hope that readers will accept that there really wasn't going to be an opportunity for me to have a bra for the duration of our stay. Ho hum.

Chapter Eight

SPEAK SWAHILI: SIMBA – LION

Obediently, at 6.00am we had placed our luggage outside our room and were back in the sumptuous dining room, breakfasting with our fellow travellers and four guides. The last two members of the group, mother and daughter, Deb and Jill, had arrived in the small hours of the morning and had hardly any sleep. Their luggage had not arrived at all – they only had the clothes they had travelled in, but they were remarkably and admirably chirpy, putting my bralessness into perspective. Vivien had organised a chain of drivers who would locate their baggage when it arrived and get it to our destination by some means or another.

Half an hour later, at precisely 6.30am, we pulled out of the hotel car park in the customised Toyota Land Cruisers. On the days where we would be travelling long distances, Vivien had arranged that we would travel together to give us some time to catch up on the last 11 years. Our driver on these days would be Dedan, also known as 'the Professor' because of his prodigious knowledge and accompanying patience.

We were cruising down the road I had taken to school, and to and from work 6 times a week – in those days we worked on Saturday mornings – for 8 years. I could almost have driven it with my eyes closed then. Now it was unrecognisable, with nose-to-tail traffic and modern buildings where once there had just been trees. It brought back vivid memories.

I remembered clearly the first day I drove myself to work after passing my driving test. It was even more stressful than it ought to have been because I had had to pay a bribe to get my licence. As we had pulled up back at the test centre, the examiner had congratulated me, saying that I had successfully passed both the oral and practical aspects of the test. He then continued that at the point when I had done a three-point turn, if there had been a crate of beer or a bottle of whisky behind the car, I would have touched it with the bumper and might have broken it. Being very young and green, the significance of his remark passed straight over my head, and after two or three minutes silence while I tried to think of something to say, he sadly shook his head and told me I had failed.

When I reported this to my driving instructor, he laughed and said of course I had failed. Next time I should make sure there was a bottle of whisky, wrapped in a bag, on the back seat. Some money also had to change hands, as if you failed a test there was a mandatory delay before you could retake it – I think it was six months. However, there was a clerk who for a modest financial consideration could be relied upon to remove all trace of the first test from the log kept at the test centre, so I could retake the test the following week. This one I passed quickly, without having to drive. The examiner climbed into the car, glanced over his shoulder, tucked the bottle into his jacket, and asked me to read the number plate on a car parked 10 feet away. He then shook my hand vigorously and congratulated me. So although I had a driving licence, I expected at any moment to be arrested for bribery.

Driving hesitantly down the hill towards the town centre on that first day, I noticed a very large spider on the bonnet of the car, but I was concentrating fiercely on remembering how and when to change gear and took my eye off the creature. A few minutes later the traffic lights turned red, and as I braked, I saw to my horror that the spider was now in the car, on the upper corner of the windscreen nearest to me. Trying to encourage it out, I waved a book at it and (this is the almost-worst part) it reared back and stuck out two front legs as if it was planning to attack. I dropped the book and took my foot off the clutch. The car was in gear, and (this is the worst part) bumped gently into the rear of the car in front of me.

An angry European man jumped out and shouted at me, brushing aside my explanation about the spider and my first day of driving, and saying women shouldn't be allowed to drive. Luckily, there was no damage to either car. I drove to the car park, one eye on the road and the other on the spider that was huddled in what may have been either defensive or attack mode, sort of curled up as if it was likely to spring. The newspaper vendor came up as I parked, and I said 'No, thank you, I don't want a paper, but I will give you a *samuni* (50 cents) if you will take the spider out of my car.' He reached in and removed the creature, tossing it away and laughingly accepting the coin.

This incident did serve a useful purpose, however, as from then on I kept the car windows tightly shut. Driving down the same road one morning I became aware of a cyclist keeping pace with me, shouting and pulling angry faces. Maybe I had inadvertently offended him, because as we came to the lights and I braked, he unleashed a full faceful of spittle all over the windscreen. At least it didn't go in the car. It was funny how those two incidents came to mind after so many years.

We turned onto what used to be Princess Elizabeth Highway, which used to be lined with flowering trees and clouds of bougainvillea in all its colours. It's now known as Uhuru Highway, and had transformed into a crowded, scruffy road, with cattle, goats, sheep, chickens and donkeys grazing and pecking on a few withered patches of grass on the narrow central reservation. It looked as if some effort was being made to rectify this, but the overall impression was of devastation.

Where at one time there had been relatively few cars on the highway and the majority of people either walked or cycled, cars were jammed bumper-to-bumper and at all angles, while raggedly-dressed men heaved and dragged overloaded wooden handcarts around them. Morose marabou storks, nature's refuse collectors, perched in the trees, and the bridges over the road were festooned with clothing for sale. Wherever there was space, nurserymen displayed beautiful plants in black polythene bags, neatly arranged by the roadside. There were so many people! Thousands of pedestrians walking to work, and looking almost certain to arrive long before passengers trapped in the gridlocked cars and buses. Everyone appeared to be talking on their mobile phone.

The *askari* who once stood on a small platform to direct the traffic, smart in his uniform, had been replaced by traffic lights, which were not working. A couple of harried policemen waved their arms ineffectually, while drivers ignored them, intent only on going where they wanted to go, by whatever means and route they could find.

The roads and buildings were covered in advertising posters promoting properties for sale, internet providers, exhibitions, churches, schools, electronics, luxury goods. It was noisy and crowded and the quiet, orderly little colonial town I had left behind had become a boom town. All this frenetic, enthusiastic activity, and the sun was barely up.

Our convoy kept calm and carried on. By the time we reached the outskirts of the town, the traffic had begun to thin out and become less chaotic. Over the years industrial development has extended for miles beyond the original town boundary, expanding ominously right into Nairobi National Park at the expense of the wild animals who live there.

Once-barren areas had disappeared beneath new villages, bypasses, vast, sophisticated shopping malls and market stalls. The potholes, corrugations, dust or mud that once represented the road had been transformed into a ribbon of silky smooth tarmac, and the old names that are pleasing to the tongue were still comfortingly familiar: Kileleshwa, Ngong, Langata, Embakasi even if their faces were unrecognisable.

Boda boda taxis

Another striking change was in the local transport sphere. In isolated rural areas at one time the local 'taxi service' used to be a pedal bicycle called a *boda boda*, where the passenger perched on a cushion on the luggage rack behind the rider. Given the state of the roads at the time – many of them nothing more than rough tracks – I could not imagine what hard work it must have been for the rider, let alone how uncomfortable it was for the passenger. Even with the modern, geared bike I had as a teenager, riding it over lumpy ground was exhausting. The new prosperity has enabled *boda boda* drivers to replace their bikes with motorcycles, which they lovingly pimp with magnificent artwork. At the roadside, drivers lounged against their polished machines chatting to each other while they awaited passengers. We passed one dressed as Spiderman, complete with a face mask – quite a sight!

Also consigned to history along with the pedal bike taxies were the lethal *matatus* of the 1960s, Peugeot station wagons, or estate cars as we called them, whose capacity was sufficiently flexible that no passenger was ever turned away. They just kept cramming in, climbing on top of, or hanging onto. Europeans almost never travelled in these things, but I'd unavoidably had to on a memorable occasion in which 12 of us were jammed in, with baskets of fruit and vegetables and a wooden cage of chickens. They were driven with terrifying panache and total disregard for maintenance, the highway code, personal safety or other road users. Seldom if ever serviced, they were liable to collapse in a heap without warning. But the fares were cheap. And life was cheap.

The *matatus* are more regulated now, owned and operated by local co-operatives – Saccos. Like the motorbikes many of them are superbly decorated, and often include wifi facilities as well as piped music. The *As You Like It Safaris* fleet of Land Cruisers are licensed as public service vehicles, which are restricted to 50mph in an attempt to reduce Kenya's alarmingly poor record in road safety. While it's a good idea, it made our long journeys hard work for our guides who were all expert drivers.

A large sign announced: 'You are entering a corruption-free zone. Do not pay any money. Giving and receiving bribes is an offence.' Dedan snorted.

The last time I had driven past Athi River it had been a desolate place where there was pretty much nothing apart from the *Kenya Meat Commission* abattoir. Now as we approached I saw that the area is dominated by a large cement plant and surrounded by a small town of luxury properties.

The road forked, the left leading to Machakos, the right to Kajiado, two names from the past that brought a lump to my throat and heart, both a physical sensation and a kaleidoscope of shifting images causing conflicting memories of joy and loss.

As a young teenager, my happiest days were spent on a cattle ranch belonging to a young English dairy-farming family who supplemented their income by hosting children during the school holidays. They lived at a small place called Konza in the Machakos district. It was a 40-mile drive from our home in Nairobi, on the Mombasa road which at that time comprised of corrugations of red dust, or red sticky mud depending on the season. Further south was the additional hazard of elephants who sometimes liked to stand on the edge of the road flapping their ears and shaking their heads to warn cars not to pass. As far as I recall, the whole 300-mile road was only surfaced with tarmac at some time during the mid-1960s. I think that was for the benefit of Mzee Jomo Kenyatta to travel to his coastal home, because he was unable to fly due to high blood pressure. It certainly made travelling to Mombasa a great deal quicker and more comfortable, but it took away the sense of adventure.

The landscape then was speckled with scrubby bushes and rocky outcrops, populated by great herds of zebra, giraffe and an abundance of antelope – kongoni, Grant's and Thomson's gazelles. Life on the farm was bliss. We lived in total freedom, swimming in boreholes, riding the hunters and polo ponies, playing cowboys and Indians in the bushes. There was only one rule: never point a gun, loaded or unloaded, at anybody. The house had no electricity, and the cook prepared our food in a separate building on a charcoal stove. When night fell, he lit the kerosene lamps that were our only form of illumination. Evenings were spent playing games in front of an open fire.

I didn't realise it at the time, but we were living the last few years of Kenya as a British colony. Many of the white settlers were from the British aristocracy, second sons with no prospects of inheritance of the family fortune, who had come to this land as pioneers. The family where we stayed was one, the son's father a baronet who lived a short way down the hill. They were charming, gentle and slightly eccentric people who had come to Kenya long ago, having walked or travelled by ox cart hundreds of miles to set up their homes. Their house was filled with antique furniture and rugs, oil paintings of glaring ancestors, big game trophies. They maintained their lifestyle with uniformed servants who served dinner in the dining room with its polished mahogany table and chairs, silverware and fine china. Behind this Downton Abbey façade the reality of life was quite different, as they had to overcome diseases both of themselves and of livestock, illness, injuries, drought, flood, pest, wild animals and occasionally native attacks. Life wasn't easy in the early days as pioneers, despite their apparent wealth and comfort, but their breeding required that they must keep up appearances. They knew how to let their hair down, though. I remember evenings spent watching in astonishment and glee as the local farmers dressed in ladies' nightdresses to ride midnight steeplechases, and sang bawdy songs at the polo club, revealing that adults were really just children who had grown up.

Seeing the sign to Machakos brought back so many memories, and a pang of grief, because after two years of those idyllic holidays the husband of the family was killed in a motor accident, and that was the end of those halcyon days. Although that was more than 50 years ago, it is still at the front of my mind. I was inconsolable. It was my first experience of losing somebody I cared about. I was perpetually in tears, not only at the loss of a person I had loved, but at the loss of everything that Machakos meant to me.

Now the little dusty cluster of Konza had been earmarked for development into a multi-million-pound project to build a technology city, Kenya's answer to Silicon Valley, and I supposed all memories of the past would be buried beneath it.

To anybody who didn't live in Kenya in those days, it's difficult to describe just how extraordinary life was, although at the time it didn't feel extraordinary. It felt entirely normal. Many people kept exotic pets – bush babies, cheetah, orphaned deer. I remember visiting a family who had a monkey that perched above the front door and urinated on guests as they came in. At the vet's, I sat next to a lady who had a chimpanzee dressed in a T-shirt and little grey shorts. He used the family toilet just like a human, she told me proudly. There was nothing unusual about having ants in the sugar bowl, geckos running around on the ceiling, snakes in the garden or occasionally the house. It was no surprise when the bathwater came out of the taps dark brown after heavy rain. You shook the biscuit tin to dislodge the weevils, and sifted your flour to extract them. We wore elephant hair bracelets, never questioning where they came from. Khaki was the colour worn by 'old Kenya' folk, with wide-brimmed hats often trimmed with leopard skin, and chukka boots. It was like living on a film set.

Kenyans were employed as domestic cooks, gardeners, nannies, grooms, paid what by our standards was a very small wage, but by their standards, and for their needs, a comfortable one. We provided housing, staple food items, charcoal for cooking, and general care for them and their families who often came to stay. They, in turn, worked for us willingly and with enormous generosity of spirit, accepting each other's foibles and idiosyncrasies. They were part of the family. I think that for we Europeans that era was the very best. We led such a hedonistic lifestyle with the benefit of all that cheap labour. When we weren't at work we simply enjoyed ourselves. We didn't need to cook or clean or garden or wash the car. It was all done for us, leaving us free to have fun. Nairobi's mild climate was reliably predictable so you could plan outings without fear that they'd be rained off. Local food was of the highest quality, and it was cheap. If you wanted to invite friends for a meal, or throw a party, it was easy. You told the cook what you wanted and for how many, and he did the cooking, serving, clearing up and cleaning. Life was so easy and carefree.

Machakos held another significance, too. As a new young wife I had not a clue how to cook, clean or run a house – something I had never had to do. Our incumbent in the early days was Peter, willing and enthusiastic, but with housekeeping skills only slightly ahead of mine, and he could only make two dishes – omelette, or as he called it 'mombletti', – and a dense soggy little pellet that he described as 'cakey' and which he cooked in the pressure cooker. Cooking really wasn't his forte but he was extremely polite and tried so hard that I hadn't had the heart to let him go, while wondering how long we could continue eating momblettis and cakey. I was trying to learn to cook when I came home from work, and together we made a mess in the kitchen, and sometimes things turned out, but mostly they didn't. Luckily, my mother-in-law was a wonderful cook – I have never eaten better Italian food since – but we couldn't keep going to her house to eat.

I was floundering until a family friend arrived one day and asked if I needed a cook, saying that that he had somebody with him who would change my life. I didn't need any persuasion, and that is how Mwiba Ngui came to join our household.

He was a tall man with a huge smile that filled his eyes, always barefoot and spotlessly dressed in khaki shorts and a clean white shirt. For the next five years, he looked after every aspect of our lives.

Peter was relocated to the garden where he was at his happiest and where his talents were were only marginally better than his cooking skills.

After Mwiba's arrival the house always smelled faintly of polish, freshly ironed linen and aromas of delicious food. He could turn out a perfect English roast with crisp, fluffy potatoes and towering Yorkshire puddings, authentic Indian curries and Italian food that rivalled my mother-in-law's. He adored the children and our pets, dealing with all their quirks and injuries with tolerance and tenderness.

Mwiba was from the Kamba tribe, and returned to his family home at Machakos twice a year and for weekends, always coming back with a gift, usually a great basket of fruit or vegetables, once a chicken, and once a lamb. Both the latter ended up on our table, although I did not realise it until I noticed they were no longer around. Even as a meat-eater at the time, I was still averse to eating anything that I had fed.

Mwiba was at the heart of our family for five years, always smiling, always willing, with a huge capacity for love, a beautiful person. I regret that I lost contact with him once I left Kenya. He would be quite an old man now; I wished I could see him again, and liked to think that he was retired and enjoying a peaceful life in his village in Machakos.

After the road accident that put an end to my stays on the farm, I felt that I would never smile again, until the day some months later that I noticed an advertisement in the local newspaper. 'Horse wanted for 14-year-old girl', and I knew that the girl was me. My long dream of having my own pony was going to come true.

There were three replies to the advertisement. Two were local to where we lived, the third was 40 miles away, in Kajiado. Unlike the wrinkle-free road we were now driving on, I could still vividly remember the dusty, bumpy drive there in 1961 to meet the Darling family, with my fingernails digging into my palms, my jaw clenched so tight that it ached, hardly breathing. At my first sight of a bright-eyed, flea-bitten, grey pony, I felt my heart melt, as it did again then and still does now, remembering the velvet softness of her nose, the fringes of hair on her ears, the intelligence and alertness in her brown eyes and the sweet smell of warm horse. It was overwhelming love at first sight, before I had sat on her. Even though she carted me off at a smart gallop before I was ready, I knew that I had found my perfect horse.

Is a horse lover's first horse the same as the first lover, the one you remember most? Tears stung my eyes as I remembered those days, that moment, so long ago. I felt a terrible yearning to be taken back there.

I had never expected that all these memories would come flooding back. I was quite shaken.

Chapter Nine

SPEAK SWAHILI: TEMBO – ELEPHANT

We'd been driving for an hour when we had a puncture. While Terry and Michael, our co-passenger, helped Dedan to fix it, a small group of children gathered to watch, seemingly fascinated and greatly enjoying the sight of *wazungu* getting their hands dirty.

Our first destination was the Amboseli National Park, 140 miles south of Nairobi. With our speed limited to the mandatory 50mph, we settled down to sit back and enjoy the journey. Each of the custom built Land Cruisers was well equipped for long journeys, with numerous power points for recharging camera batteries, tablets and laptops, as well as giant beanbags for camera supports and bottles of refrigerated mineral water, boiled sweets and a selection of ginger and Digestive biscuits (which when we're being silly we call 'suggestive' biscuits). The pop-up roofs were designed to enable passengers to stand up comfortably for game spotting and photographing, while giving protection from the sun. A supply of colourful red *shukas* – the Maasai traditional blankets – were available to cover passengers from dust, sun or the chilly early mornings.

The smooth, wide road was built by the Chinese who are heavily invested in developing Kenya's infrastructure. There has been much criticism of Chinese influence and cries of: 'The Chinese are exploiting Africa,' as if Africa hasn't always been exploited. For its mineral wealth – look at that big hole in Kimberley where native South Africans worked in inhuman conditions to bring diamonds to the surface. Copper, slaves, ivory, gemstones, labour, timber, animals –

does it actually make any difference to Africans who exploits them? At least now the roads are passable in all weathers. I've read a great deal of outrage about Chinese workers killing and eating wildlife, while Europeans and Americans have been killing wildlife for pleasure for more than a hundred years. I'm not at all political, that's just my personal view on who has done what to Africa.

We'd been driving for almost three hours when the fuzzy grey outline of the Namanga Hills – Ol Doinyo Orok mountain as it is called by the Maasai – poked up into a hazy blue sky, and we pulled into the car park of a curio shop where those in need could find a lavatory. It's a clever marketing ploy to provide toilets at these places, because generally there are no other opportunities for very long distances unless you fancy taking your chances behind a bush. To reach the loos you have to walk through the shop, and who knows, you may be tempted to buy something from the displays of carvings, paintings, fabrics and jewellery. So the facilities aren't up to the standard of a 5-star hotel, but they were not that bad; I'd seen worse in France 30 years ago. A smiling man with a mop and bucket was swilling disinfectant around on the floor, and pushed open the door for me with a flourish. Back on the road again, we turned off a short distance before the Tanzanian border onto a road untouched by Chinese influence; a bona fide Kenyan road surface of pale dust, lumpy rocks, pot holes and rigid bone-rattling corrugations.

Vivien and I started laughing simultaneously as we bounced around. This was travel as we remembered it from decades ago, when every journey was an adventure into the unknown. On the farm at Machakos all those years ago we drove around in a Land Rover whose rear seats were metal boxes where tools and guns were kept, so when we hit bumps or bounced down into the steep gulleys we called *dongas*, our heads would hit the vehicle's roof, and our backsides and legs were permanently speckled black and blue with bruises.

On this rough road, the final forty miles to our lodge took almost two hours, and once we settled into the rhythm it felt like a high-speed total body massage. The cushions and well-sprung chassis ensured that while our journey was bouncy, it was not uncomfortable, at least for the passengers. For the drivers, it was hard work.

Have you ever seen a photograph of Amboseli National Park that didn't feature Mount Kilimanjaro? The funny thing is that the two are in different countries – Amboseli is in Kenya, while Mount Kilimanjaro, Africa's highest mountain, is in neighbouring Tanzania. If you look at a map showing the border between the two countries, while it runs straight as an arrow for most of its 477 miles, there is a noticeable kink in the area of Mount Kilimanjaro. There is a legend/apocryphal tale that Queen Victoria 'gave' Kilimanjaro to her grandson, Kaiser Wilhelm II, when the East African Protectorate was being carved up between England and Germany, so that Britain would 'have' Mount Kenya and Germany would 'have' Kilimanjaro. While it's an entertaining tale, I don't believe there is any factual evidence to back it up.

Amboseli comes from the word e*mbusel* meaning salty and dusty in Maa, the language of the Maasai people, and it certainly applies to this sun-bleached, wind-baked, gritty stage, where whirlwinds twirled like phantoms in an ethereal dance across the plains. Everything was covered in veils of pale dust created by the volcanic ash that makes up the topsoil of Amboseli. I wondered how this barren landscape could support life. Yet it did, for we began to pass herds of plump Grant's and Thomson's gazelles, wildebeeste and zebras, families of sharp-eyed baboons, and warthogs rooting in the soil. These animals can manage without water for a long time, obtaining the moisture they need from the leaves they eat – not that there seemed to be many of those –

and from night-time dew.

Ahead of us, a small figure herded a few cattle to drink from a murky puddle beside the road. When the animals had finished, the figure squatted down and began to scoop up the water into his mouth with his hands. Michael cried out in dismay: 'Don't drink that!' and waved a bottle of mineral water taken from the cooler. What looked like a little grey-haired old man trotted up to us, wearing ill-fitting clothes and shoes made from old tyres. As he reached out to take the bottle, we could see that he was no more than a young boy, his hair and skin covered in the white dust. He took the bottle without comment and drank thirstily, and then stopped at the vehicle behind us where Ken, one of our group, also gave him a bottle that he jammed into his pocket before shuffling away through the dust and back to his herd.

Away to our left was a line of trees behind a lush green area with large grey blobs in it. It was a little too far to see clearly with the naked eye, but with my telephoto lens I could see eight hippo slumbering peacefully in the marshes. Coming from their right were a dozen elephants of varying sizes slowly advancing upon them to serve an eviction notice. I wondered whether the lodgers were going to put up any resistance, but they went peacefully, heaving themselves onto their fat legs and ambling away. It was so long since I'd seen elephants in their natural habitat, and even though they were far away, I was thrilled.

At the entrance to Amboseli Lodge are two stone pillars with a row of thin plaited ropes stretched between them and dangling down, like a primitive threadbare car wash. They brushed against the vehicle as we drove through. I asked Dedan why they were there. 'To stop the elephants,' he replied. I thought he was joking, but Vivien confirmed that it does indeed deter them from coming into the grounds and trampling on the flowerbeds. It didn't look much of a deterrent to anything but apparently elephants don't like it and it is very effective.

Almost before the vehicles stopped, porters had unloaded our bags and were leading the way to our rooms, through winding stone paths bordered by raised beds of succulent plants in shades of green and purple, and towering trees where birds sang and monkeys played. Our accommodation was in small bungalows camouflaged among the trees to have the minimum visual impact on the environment. The room was immaculately clean, bright and sunny, the yellow and ochre walls painted with an exquisite landscape mural. Deep rich reds and blue soft furnishings added an exotic touch, while the huge bed sported blinding white linen and was entirely enclosed by a 'tent' of mosquito netting. The modern bathroom was spotless and stocked with toiletries and big fluffy towels.

Sliding glass doors led onto a private verandah overlooking lawns and trees. 'Don't leave them open when you leave your room,' advised our porter. 'The monkeys will come in!'

Indeed the bands of vervet monkeys were watching us from up in the trees, among the shrubs, and on the grass, studying us intently with their bright little eyes. It was only a few minutes before shouts of laughter nearby signalled that a marauding monkey had dashed into one of our group's rooms and escaped with several packets of sugar and a bar of chocolate from the tea tray.

We sat on our verandah with a cup of coffee, enjoying the warmth of the sun and the sounds and smells of Africa that I had missed and dreamt of for so long. After all the travelling, I felt that I really was finally back in the Kenya I love. The monkeys continued watching us closely. When we pretended that we were falling asleep, and closed our eyes, they crept silently forward and leapt onto the table, rushing away if we made the slightest movement. Brightly coloured agama lizards sunbathed on the warm stones, watching with unblinking eyes, ready to dart away in their strange, stiff-legged gait if we went too close. I couldn't remember a time I had felt more content and relaxed. If we were rich, I think we could have happily lived there forever.

To reach the dining room, you walk from the lobby over a wooden bridge spanning a little stream. There's a Maasai *moran* who stands at the entrance, dressed in tribal costume and carrying a spear and *seme* – the traditional Maasai knife – on his belt. I didn't think it at all likely that we would be invaded by man or beast with any evil intent, but it was comforting to know he was there if we needed him.

Lunch was served buffet-style, with a feast of fresh meats and fish cooked to order, salads, curries with all their traditional accompaniments, and fragrant freshly-baked bread rolls. To go with the selection of cheeses there were chutneys and pickles, followed by a large choice of elaborate desserts – gateaux, ice creams, flans, tarts, soufflés, mousses and flambées. Looking at the baskets of fresh fruits – pineapple, watermelon, oranges, mangoes, papaya – I could see in my mind, an avocado tree surrounded by fallen fruits left to rot, the mango, loquat, guava and papaya trees and a hedge of passion fruit, barely touched when they grew in my garden. Terry asked if they were the same fruits that we buy in France – not that often because they are all luxury items. Yes, I answered, 'they are the same, why do you ask?' Because, he replied, they taste so different. They taste of sunshine. They smell sweeter, their colours are brighter, their flesh juicier.

He was right. There is no comparison between food eaten in its place of birth and travel-weary produce. It just doesn't taste the same.

Our group of 16 shared a table. Mother and daughter, Deb and Jill; Californians Tom and Peggy; from Seattle Bob and Beth; Mike and Stacey, animal lovers like us; photographer

Ken and his Kiwi partner Jessica; Cindy, the most travelled person I'd ever met; Jim, a retired military pilot, Vivien and her partner, Michael, and ourselves. Any initial worries I had about fitting in with the group had disappeared. They were all friendly, sophisticated people and immediately made us feel welcome.

At a nearby table, our four guides were seated together having lunch, and I wondered what they were talking about. Were they exchanging opinions about their new passengers, and if so, what did they think of us? I'd love to have eavesdropped. I knew from talking to them that tourists are a mixed bunch, varied in their character and behaviour. There are those who care about the wildlife and conservation while others have no interest at all and misbehave, shouting at the animals, feeding them with sweets, leaving litter and smoking in the reserves. However difficult these people are, the guides have to hide their distaste and try to educate them into how to behave properly. Whatever our guides may think of our group, I am certain they have nothing to fear regarding our behaviour. Except for me. There's always the possibility I may disgrace myself towards the end of our stay.

Chapter Ten

SPEAK SWAHILI: NYATI – BUFFALO

Our first game drive wasn't until 4.00pm, when the heat of the afternoon was subsiding, so we had a couple of hours to relax. Although the pool looked cool and inviting, I felt as big as a walrus and feared that if I got in there would be no room for the water, so instead we sat outside our bungalow listening to the birds and watching the monkeys watching us.

When we set off later it was warm and hazy, and Kilimanjaro was hidden behind cloud. I didn't expect that we would see much in the way of wildlife either in this barren landscape that did not look as if it could support any life form apart from reptiles and insects.

But we began to see large herds of zebra and wildebeeste together, all plump and glossy as they scraped around among the withered scrub in the dust, and I was wondering how they managed on an apparent diet of grit and dead wood, when we arrived at a marshy area fed by the snow melt from the mountain, where herds stood fetlock-deep in the water, grazing lush grass.

I have always loved the wildebeeste, or gnu. They are one of my favourite beasts with their glossy metallic pelts, their wise beards and the way they will suddenly kick up their heels, bucking, running, twisting and turning, just for fun.

Wildebeeste are antelope, Dedan remarked. An antelope is a mammal that chews the cud and has hollow horns that grow throughout its lifetime. They typically have large ears and eyes and a keen sense of smell to warn them of predators. He pointed to a nearby group of elegant impala, supreme jumpers that are unique among antelope because of a tuft of black hair on the back of their heels. When a herd is under attack they will scatter to confuse their attackers, and the very young are left behind. Those tufts of hair cover a gland which releases a scent that will enable the herd to regroup and the young to find their mothers when danger has passed.

Dedan

The impala are sometimes known as 'fast food', because they're fast, they are food for the big cats, and they have a black stripe down centre of their tails, and a slightly curved, black stripe either side, like brackets, which is similar to the McDonald's arched 'M' logo.

Nearby were some Thomson's gazelles with their long, pointed horns and the distinctive thick, black stripe running up their sides. While all gazelles are antelopes, not all antelopes are gazelles, Dedan continued. That sounded like the beginning of one of those mental agility tests that I can never work out. Gazelles are generally smaller than antelope, and both sexes have horns unlike their larger relatives where female horns are rare. We'd only been driving ten minutes and I'd already learned several things. What antelope do have in common, apart from their sheer elegance and beauty, is stotting. They both stot.

A couple of crested cranes were showing off to each other, demonstrating their particular acrobatic skills. One was leaping into the air and landing with its wings dramatically raised (reminding me of a ballet dancer); the other balanced on one leg looking unimpressed. They are beautiful, flamboyant birds. Long ago, a friend raised one she had rescued as an abandoned chick. It was a curious bird that took an interest in everything shiny, and used to entertain itself pecking at my watch. One day, I leaned down and it struck with the speed of a snake straight at my eye. Luckily, I was wearing sunglasses otherwise I'd probably have been wearing a black patch now.

In case you are wondering about stotting, it is leaping vertically into the air somewhat like Nureyev performing a grand jeté.

'Look! A pack of hyenas,' I cried. They are unfortunate animals with a bad reputation. It's true that in the nursery there is some nasty behaviour as the young fight for supremacy and murder their siblings, but I find them attractive in their own way. They have a handsome canine head, a rich spotted fur, and a purposeful, sexy slink to their walk.

'It is a clan. The collective noun for a group of hyenas is a clan,' corrected Dedan. 'These are spotted hyenas. *Crocuta crocuta*. They are also called laughing hyenas, but they are not laughing; when you hear that noise it is because they are angry. The striped hyenas are more timid, and they do not vocalise so loudly.'

He continued. 'Hyenas are both hunters and scavengers, opportunists, and theirs is a matriarchal society; the females are larger, and dominate the males.' From his tone, I deduced he didn't think much of that. He's a Kikuyu man. Although cubs are born precocial, their mothers will nurse them for a year or even longer. When they are a few weeks old, the mothers move their cubs into group 'nurseries', using underground dens dug and abandoned by other animals.'

I quickly jotted down 'precocial' in my notebook, having no idea what it meant or even how to spell it, but not wanting to appear ignorant I scribbled 'pre-co-shal'. I'd look it up later.

While all our attention was on the hyenas in front of us, my camera battery ran out, and I turned around to take a new one from my bag. I caught my breath and froze, because ten feet behind us, three elephants – a juvenile and a female with her small baby – were plodding towards us through the dust, like giant earth-moving machines. I had been expecting and longing to see elephants, but somehow I hadn't anticipated them being quite so close. Were they meant to be there? Did our guide even know?

As I turned I caught Dedan's eye in the wing mirror. It showed a faint hint of amusement. He switched off the engine and we stood motionless as the animals passed as silently as shadows and so close that we could have reached out and touched them without stretching. They were so, so majestic and beautiful. The baby was less than a year old, still small enough to walk beneath its mother's belly. Its tusks would not begin to show until it was about 18 months. The group stopped a little way ahead, and while we were watching the mother feeding her calf, six other adult elephants had appeared behind us and they too were within an arm's length. We were standing up on the seats, looking out through the pop-up roof, level with their eyes, and I could count every individual wiry eyelash as they brushed lightly against the sides of the vehicle, and in their eyes lay the wisdom of the universe.

One of them seemed to have an injury to the side of its face, a patch of darkened skin that looked wet and oily. It's a secretion from a gland on their temples, between the ear and eye, and it signals a particular emotion like stress, or excitement, something seen in male elephants when they are in musth and surging testosterone levels make them aggressive. These elephants continued quietly on their peaceful way and started grazing a few yards from us.

That was the closest I'd ever been to wild elephants; I'd never imagined the possibility of being within stroking distance. They were completely calm as they grazed, kicking the tussocks with their front feet to loosen the clumps of rough, thick grass, then pulling it up with their trunks.

From the rear, both sexes look similar with a sack of loose flesh between their hind legs. It is by the shape of their heads that you can distinguish them, the females having flattened foreheads, while the males are rounded.

That reminded me of our 10-year-old daughter running into the house one day when we were entertaining elderly relatives.

'Mummy,' she yelled, 'guess what? I can tell the difference between boy horses and girl horses!'

'That's clever, darling, you must tell me LATER,' I replied.

'But Mummy...'

'LATER, darling,' I repeated. 'We are talking now.'

'But Mummy, listen!' She would not be silenced. 'The girl horses have longer eyelashes.'

I don't know how long we stayed there, in silence, entranced by the sight of these creatures so close and moving so quietly on their spongy, cushioned toes. The only sound was the despairing squeak of another trunkful of grass as it was wrenched from its moorings.

It was not until the shadows became long and thin that we drove back beneath the elephant-deterrent strings. Curfew in the park starts at 6.00pm and drivers face fines if they fail to return to the lodge by then.

I told you earlier about the Swahili way of telling the time, so you will know that 6.00pm is hour twelve of the day – *saa kumi na mbili asubuhi*. Next time the big hand reached the top of the clock it would be hour one of the night – *saa moja usiku*.

We just had time for a quick shower before meeting with the rest of our group on the verandah outside the dining room, to share our experiences and tick off in our green books the numerous wildlife we had seen during the day. Thirty feet away, the perimeter lights picked out the eyes from a herd of waterbuck moving quietly through the night.

During dinner, an unbelievably excruciating pain arrived suddenly in my right shoulder. It was so overwhelming, I felt that I might pass out. I bent and twisted and pulled and pushed it, rubbed and poked it, rotated it, shrugged it up and down, but nothing brought relief. Jim kindly gave me some strong painkillers, but they had no effect, and I spent a restless night waving my arm in the air, dangling it over the side of the bed, tucking it under my belly and behind my neck, but the pain would not go away, so I lay in the dark enjoying the sounds of the African night, chirrups and squeaks, chewing and grunts.

Chapter Eleven

SPEAK SWAHILI: CHUI – LEOPARD

Kamara was our guide for our second day in Amboseli, and we shared a vehicle with photographer Ken and Kiwi Jessica – lovely, smiley, happy people. As we left the lodge, a whirlwind enveloped us in a choking dust storm. Billowing clouds of thick grit poured through the open top of the vehicle and we had to wrap the *shukas* around our heads and faces. While Terry and I could tuck our cameras away easily inside our jackets, Ken was concerned for his much larger camera and lenses. He wanted to turn back, but Kamara continued driving through the dust devil until we came out through the other side 10 minutes later, so smothered in the white dust that we somewhat resembled ghosts.

We saw our first lions – three young adults sprawling in the long grass, still showing the rosette pattern on their bellies and legs, and the first signs of a mane on the male. Lions hunt during the cooler hours of evening, night and early morning, and as the sun slid up over the horizon they stirred, yawned and wrestled lazily with each other. Fifty yards away, a small herd of Grant's gazelle were seemingly unaware of the lions' presence. The cats rolled on their backs, stood up, nuzzled each other and laid down again, while the gazelle moved ever closer, grazing steadfastly.

The male lion sat up and began to watch them. 'Run!' I wanted to shout to the gazelle. 'Get out of here!' I didn't want to see a kill. Any kill. Predators have to eat, and it is essential for the balance of nature that the population of herbivores is controlled, but I don't enjoy seeing anything, human or animal, frightened, running for its life, or being

51

attacked and hurt. I'd seen it enough in the past. Once something is dead, that's different, but I don't want to see it happening. Still, I recognised that for many people seeing a kill was a highlight of their safari.

To my relief the lion took no notice of the gazelle, but wandered away in the opposite direction and disappeared from sight to our right. Shortly afterwards, the other two stood up and began to move away from us and we lost sight of them. Across the other side of the valley, we could see a large herd of impala and topi grazing at the edge of a copse of doum palms. They suddenly froze in unison, looked behind them and began to run and scatter. It looked as though the lions had chosen their breakfast. Rather foolishly, I felt, the gazelle who had been grazing near us galloped away towards the fleeing herds.

All through our trip I frequently felt slightly detached, as if I was floating in my own bubble of sheer contentment, only aware of our surroundings, and remote from other people. As if I was the first and only person on earth, seeing it for the first time, that this was my personal kingdom and that time was standing still. That's the best way I can describe it, almost like an out-of-body experience. Sometimes, when we were sitting in silence, I thought back to my early life here, and how I could have done things differently. That doesn't mean that I was in any way discontent with my life. I love France, it's been my home for more than 20 years, but for me nowhere will ever compare with Kenya. Hemingway wrote: 'I never knew of a morning in Africa when I woke up that I was not happy.' That is how I felt. Past difficulties were only surface blips. Inside, right in my heart, Africa had always made me happy.

There are thousands of people like me around the world who lived in Kenya and who decades after leaving are still in love with the country no matter where they are now. I knew that Terry was having an experience quite different to mine. For him it was just a holiday in a foreign place, for me it was my old home, and he couldn't be expected to feel the same love that I did, so it was fortunate that we were travelling with a group of people who were very sociable and all shared his passion for aviation in one way of another. When I was mentally away on my own, he always had company.

A lone giraffe swung its way across the dust to browse from the top of an acacia tree. Unlike the majority of four-legged animals, giraffe do not use their front and back legs diagonally, but both right legs together, and both left legs, like camels and pacer horses. I think this is what makes their locomotion so graceful. Amazingly, this splendid, beautiful and peaceable creature is now on the list of endangered species. They are being killed for bush meat and for supposed medical benefits – notably HIV and AIDS, and as man moves further into the savannah to graze cattle and grow crops, they are suffering from loss of habitat. Worst of all are the so-called trophy 'hunters' who are killing them for fun. Why would anybody find pleasure in taking the life of something beautiful, to reduce it to a heap of skin and bones?

We came across a small herd of Grant's gazelles, all alert, ears pricked, feet stamping and tails flicking.

'What are they looking at, Kamara?'

'They have seen hyena,' he replied, pointing to a slight movement among the long golden grass. Then we saw the animal, perfectly camouflaged and walking purposefully towards the gazelle. They watched it intently but apparently without alarm, as the hyena passed within three feet of them. Whatever it was doing, they understood that for the moment it was not a threat.

Although the morning was warm and sunny there was a band of low-hanging cloud and we had still not seen the top of Kilimanjaro by the time we returned to the lodge for another culinary lunchtime feast and a couple of hours of relaxation.

At 4.00pm, we drove to Observation Hill and climbed up to the top, from where there is a sweeping panorama of Africa's tallest mountain. The cloud had finally lifted revealing Africa's tallest mountain in her splendour, with the sun tingeing the icecap as it oozed down her sides like cream on a Christmas pudding.

Kilimanjaro is a relatively young mountain born out of a volcanic eruption one million years ago. It is the melt water from the mountain that fills the rivers and swamps to give life to millions of wild animals, and to humans and their livestock in this otherwise arid desert. Scientists say that over the last century Kilimanjaro has lost 82% of its ice cap. If it continues to disappear at that rate, they estimate that by 2033 there will be no more ice. If that were to happen then Amboseli would become uninhabitable for both man and wildlife. Looking down onto the great plains below, I wondered how many thousands of years it has looked like this, and how much longer it would last. I felt a terrible anxiety and sadness at the thought that it could all vanish.

However, I am a believer in the supreme power of Nature to protect our planet. Where we live in France, the ground is packed with flints and rocks just below the surface. You cannot drive a fork into the earth because it will immediately strike rock. Each time the fields are ploughed they produce a bumper crop of giant rocks, stones and flints, and you wonder how a single seed ever manages to force its way past them, let alone the hundreds of thousands of seeds that grow strong and tall into maize, or wheat, or sunflower crops. In our local village, there's a concrete pavement that butts up to the wall of a house. You couldn't put a credit card between the two, there is no apparent space. Yet, every year for as long as we have lived there, a crimson cyclamen has squeezed itself out from there and bloomed.

At Chernobyl thirty years ago, the nuclear power station

blew up and leaked radiation for thousands of miles – the fall-out was recorded in Wales. It was said the area would be uninhabitable for 3,000 years, but today it has become a haven for wolves, bears, deer and wild birds. That is why I believe that Mother Nature is invincible and I am putting my money on her to save Amboseli.

Kamara

Once we had climbed back down to the vehicles, Kamara parked beside the great green swamplands where an obese hippo and her inflated infant browsed in the shallows, and several dozen elephants stood up to their bellies in the water. Two tiny babies floundered as the water reached their ears, and their trunks poked up like periscopes, searching for help. When he saw that one was almost totally submerged and seemed to be struggling, Terry announced that he was ready to go into the water and help it. How he imagined he could help a baby elephant up to the top of its head in water, surrounded by a dozen adult elephants, was a matter for speculation. I'd once seen him dive into a swimming pool, fully dressed in a designer suit and hand-made shoes to rescue a drowning owl, so I wouldn't have put it past him. Kamara looked a little uneasy at the prospect and cautioned patience. The baby's groping trunk eventually found and wrapped itself around its mother's tail, and she moved forward guiding the baby to shallower water.

The elephants didn't have all the swamp to themselves. There was also a large herd of buffalo, carrying their passengers and hygienists, the ox-peckers, or tick-birds as we used to call them. These buff-coloured birds are about the size of a European starling, with red beaks and yellow-rimmed eyes that give them a wide-eyed and wondrous expression. They have a symbiotic relationship with the buffalo who allow them access to every part of their bodies including their ears, eyes, mouths and noses, so the birds can remove and feast upon the blood-sucking parasites that are their main diet and a source of discomfort to their hosts. Ugh. I'm so glad I'm not an ox-pecker. Snowy white egrets prowled around the animals' feet, jabbing in the wet grass at the insects and amphibians disturbed from the mud.

In his soft, slow voice Kamara described how elephants are a keystone species, essential to the eco-system and safeguarding the environment for other species. The trees they destroy make space for grass to grow. The seeds they eat are excreted to produce new trees, and when they dig for water they create depressions in the ground that will create waterholes for smaller animals during the rainy seasons. Elephants digest less than half the vast quantities of food they eat each day – grasses, leaves, bushes, bark, in fact any vegetation they can find, so their dung is particularly rich in fibre. The dung not only provides a warm and a well-provisioned home for various insects, which in turn provide a nutritious meal for small mammals, but it has created a new industry for local entrepreneurs, producing paper, and decreasing deforestation.

That evening my shoulder reached a peak of pain that tore at it like a giant pincer. I couldn't find any reason for it. It didn't hurt during the day, it didn't affect my use of the camera, but as soon as we sat down in the evening it flared up again. Poor Ken had damaged his finger slamming it in the door of the vehicle, and Vivien had called the doctor to see us.

He was a tall and very gentle, quietly-spoken man who prescribed some pain killers and went away to the dispensary to collect them. He returned twenty minutes later with a box of tablets. For his time and the medicine, all he charged was a couple of dollars.

Chapter Twelve

SPEAK SWAHILI: VIFARU – RHINO

After two days in Amboseli, we were up once more at horrible o'clock, had eaten breakfast and were ready to roll at 6.00am.

The guides were waiting at their vehicles which were polished and tidied. '*Bonjour*,' said Dedan, '*Comment ça va?*' Through their years working as guides for different nationalities, they had all picked up other languages, mostly French, Italian and German (apparently they were not keen on German as a language), and Steve had mentioned casually that he had been to college to study Japanese in order to communicate with Japanese clients. I like studying languages but have always balked at one that requires the learning of an entirely different alphabet. 'Wasn't it very difficult?' I asked. No, not really, he said. In fact, it was relatively easy as many Japanese words are similar in sound to the Luo language, although the meaning is different. So pronunciation was not a problem. Right.

Our next destination was the Mount Kenya Safari Club, 250 miles away, due north of Nairobi. To avoid the bone-shaking corrugations through the park back to Namanga, we drove eastwards to pick up the smooth Chinese-built Mombasa road. What we gained in comfort we lost in time – traffic was dense and slow.

After a couple of hours, we pulled in for a 'potty stop' at a large curio shop. Inside was a vast display of beautiful wooden and soapstone carvings, colourful fabrics and jewellery of semi-precious and mineral stones. A gentleman named Edward introduced himself, asked my name and thrust a basket into my hand. I explained that I would not be buying anything today, but he ignored that and kept picking things up and suggesting that this may be the only opportunity I would ever have to buy something so beautiful at such a bargain price. 'I can give you very, very special deals,' he said. 'You won't find such good prices anywhere else.' His persistence paid off and I asked him the price of a small ebony elephant.

'Well, you see, it depends how many things you are going to buy,' he explained. 'The more you buy, cheaper the price, you see? How many things are you going to buy today?' Unable to establish a price for the elephant, but assured that I would leave the shop happier than I entered it, and that if I bought more things the elephant's price would become almost nothing, I chose a beautiful soapstone saucer decorated with a curiously long-nosed zebra, and a shell necklace painted with the Kenyan flag, and we agreed a price which in truth was very modest for such skilled workmanship.

When I'd paid for these purchases, Edward called me over to a corner of the shop where he was carefully wrapping them in multiple sheets of newspaper and sticky tape.

'Susie,' he said quietly, quickly looking over his shoulder. (We had been on first name terms since we entered the shop.) 'Give me a little present, please. I am a most honest, hard-working man and have given you a special price. You can't buy these things anywhere else for a better price. I know you are a quality lady who appreciates service with a smile, and a man who does his job professionally. I have made you very happy, so give me 200 shillings to show that you appreciate what I have done for you.'

I slipped 200 Kenya shillings (the equivalent of 2 dollars) onto the bench and it disappeared as if by magic.

'Edward,' I said, 'you are the original silver-tongued

devil.' He chuckled, squeezed my hand in two of his, asked God to bless me, and pushed the package into my hands quickly while looking over my shoulder for a new customer on whom to work his charms.

It is a fact that wherever you travel in Kenya somebody will be trying to sell you something, by any and every means they can. It's easy to sigh and think 'Oh no, not again.' But these are just people trying to make a living. Living in remote areas, there are almost no opportunities for employment. Education is relatively recent; many have missed out. They don't have any form of social security; there is no 'dole'. There is no National Health Service. The very old and the very young are reliant on those members of the family who can find a way to earn a living and care for them. They have to feed and clothe themselves and their dependants. They live in primitive conditions without running water or electricity. That is why they are trying to sell you something – a wooden carving, a bag of potatoes, a piece of fruit, to help carrying your bags. They do it courteously and with a good-natured smile.

What is an insignificant amount to us can represent a week's security for them. It is their living. They will jump and skip in front of you, holding up their wares. They will press themselves against your vehicle and try to shove something into it – and once it's in, you are going to find it impossible to get it out. They will wave and shout and stand in front of your car. They will do anything they can to get you to buy whatever they are selling, persistently and with good humour. Picking something up to look at it is tantamount to buying it. If you are not going to buy – don't touch! And please don't scowl at them or wave them away like flies. Be generous, and if you don't buy, at least give them a smile. They are human beings, just as we are.

As we were passing back through Nairobi, I searched for familiar landmarks. Where was the drive-in cinema on Thika

Road where I went with friends every Sunday, and ate stew from a pressure cooker, and 'waterproofed' the windscreen with a cut potato if it rained? Where was Allsopps Brewery where I worked as a secretary? Where was the Spread Eagle hotel which was a favourite venue for a Sunday swim and curry lunch? Behind there was the riding school where ex-cavalry Major Blackwell taught me to ride. Bless him, he truly had the patience of a saint as it took me more than a year to learn to trot without clinging to the pommel and bouncing about in the saddle like a jelly in an earthquake. Their place had been taken by modern shopping malls.

Outside of the city there were endless shanty towns built of corrugated iron panels, schools and churches, and stalls made out of rough pieces of timber and plastic sheets. No matter how wobbly and lopsided the stalls, their products were carefully and artistically arranged: potatoes, onions, tomatoes, garlic, oranges and bananas, piled into neat pyramids, and slices of fresh pineapple hygienically wrapped in plastic. Those with nothing else to sell stood beside the road offering bottled water and soft drinks. Wherever there were small towns, there were makeshift shops (not lingerie shops, in case you are wondering), hotels and bustling markets. This was such a different Kenya to the one I remembered, when you could drive for many miles without seeing a human being.

I noticed that everywhere we went there were signs for M-Pesa. I guessed it was something to do with money, as *pesa* is the Swahili word for money. I asked Dedan to explain it. 'It is mobile money. You can use it to send cash to people and to pay your bills with your mobile phone. I'll show you later,' he replied.

He drove with calm, grim determination as time ticked away and we were two hours behind schedule. Not only did he have to ensure that our convoy stayed together through the chaotic and unpredictable traffic, but we were frequently brought to a halt by barriers constructed from hefty chunks of wood embedded with long metal spikes and placed across the road by the traffic police, more commonly known as the TKK – *toa kitu kidogo* – 'give me a little something,' meaning a bribe. I understood that the *kitu kidogo* is indeed a small thing, too small for anybody to argue over, and therefore paid pragmatically. At the end of the day, all those *kitu kidogos* will have augmented the traffic policemen's meagre salary. As a safari vehicle we seemed immune, but every other public or private vehicle and truck was stopped.

Northwards through the central highlands the landscape changed from red soil to black, past coffee plantations and groves of mangos and far more cultivation than I remembered. Nyeri, Naro Moru and Nanyuki were all names familiar to me from the distant past, and now unrecognisable. From time to time, through gaps in the trees or rounding a bend, we caught a glimpse of Mount Kenya, with her filigree shawl of snow draped around her shoulders.

Dedan's phone rang. His wife was calling to tell him her father had just died. Surely he'd want to go home to be with her, but he said that she knew he was working, and would manage on her own when she buried her father in a few days time.

We hadn't seen many – or in fact any cemeteries, and I asked him where people are usually buried. Africans, he said, are generally buried on their own land, except for unknown people who are buried in cemeteries.

With all the delays it was mid-afternoon by the time we reached the Mount Kenya Safari Club and our guides had been driving for almost nine hours. Forewarned, the club had kept lunch going for us. As well as the usual extravagant buffets, roast meats and curries there was fresh trout from the nearby river and typical Kenyan fare – *ugali* – a coarse maize meal porridge that I love and had last eaten when Mwiba shared his lunch with me almost 50 years ago, and the collard greens they call *sukuma wiki* – meaning literally 'to stretch or push the week' – that are a staple of the Kenyan diet, a cheap and nutritious addition to the weekly food budget. I didn't remember it being on the menu when I was last there in the 1960s, but since then the client base had changed and there were now many Kenyan families staying here.

Despite its name, Mount Kenya Safari Club is more hotel than club now. Once it was one of the world's most exclusive establishments where membership was solely by invitation. Now anybody who can afford it can stay here and enjoy a touch of celebrity lifestyle. In a sublime setting, it stands in green lawns surrounded by flowering trees, against the glorious backdrop of Kirinyaga, the sacred mountain of the Kikuyu tribe and home of their spiritual god, Ngai. Not quite as tall as Kilimanjaro, but every bit as majestic, Mount Kenya pushes her pointed peaks up through the forest, over the clouds and into the bluest sky, where eagles glide. The fact that she stands precisely on the equator gives her a special magic, and I think she is one of the greatest natural wonders of the world.

The club has been a favourite haunt of film stars, royalty, the rich, famous and beautiful since it was established in the 1950s by Hollywood film stars William Holden and Robert Ryan. Everybody who is anybody has stayed there at some time. It's pure class, the architecture and decor colonial style at its very best, spacious, elegant, luxurious and discreetly comfortable and all in the best possible taste. There are wildlife trophies hanging from the walls, and the huge pair of elephant tusks framing the entrance to the bar – which straddles the equator – reminders that before they became conservationists, Holden and his friend were keen hunters. These trophies were the only slight blot on an otherwise idyllic location.

If we were wealthy, I'd furnish our house like this –

without the trophies.

After lunch, we all walked down to the club's animal orphanage, past a lugubrious marabou stork. When they are not eating, they often stand in a weary hunch-backed posture like an elderly waiter who hasn't been given a decent tip, and giving the impression that they bear all the cares of the world upon their feathered shoulders.

The road was lined with brilliant blue and purple morning glories clambering up trees, showers of pink bougainvillea, pastel blue hydrangeas, exotic strelizias – the Bird of Paradise plants – flowering banana plants, many other flora I had never seen before, and poinsettias towering over our heads.

I wonder who first described Africa as the 'Dark Continent'. Anybody who has been there knows that Africa is radiant; the bluest skies, the greenest foliage, the richest and most varied colours in the world of the animals, birds and insects; the glossy yellow of pineapple, the deep orange of papaya; the pale turquoise of the waves that tickle the silver sands of the coast; the rich red of the murram and the warm, soft beige of the desert. The golden glow of the sun rising and setting on the snowcaps of the great mountains. Where is the darkness?

At the orphanage, a beaming lady named Ester introduced herself. She was responsible for the flourishing kitchen garden that grows greenery, fruit and vegetables for the orphanage residents. Petite, in a headscarf, green military style jumper and Wellington boots, with a huge smile, she proudly showed us around the numerous beds of plants in neat, orderly rows and the climbing vines and fruit trees, explaining how she rotates the crops and experiments with new ones, and pointing out which of the animals like a particular plant.

Once we'd completed our tour of her empire, she took us to meet James Muraya, the Orphanage Supervisor who is more commonly known as Elephant Man, who would be our guide around the orphanage where he had been working for twenty years. As there were no elephants there, we were intrigued by his name. I'll tell you all about it in a while – he is a very rare and unusual person.

All the wildlife at the orphanage has either been rescued from the wild, or is being bred there to increase their numbers and save them from extinction, among them the white zebra and the magnificent, rare bongo with its deep golden hide and creamy stripes.

Up on a high shelf, a rock hyrax lay doing what rock hyrax do best – sunbathing with an expression of dozy contentment on its furry face, one eye watching us with mild interest. We followed Elephant Man around the shaded grounds as he pointed out the various residents. Crested cranes strutted importantly and bongos and bushbuck grazed in the shade beside small streams. It was like a scene from Jungle Book, with the animals all around us.

We had entertained an ostrich with its broken leg in plaster, letting it stare hypnotically into our eyes and peck nuts from our heads, and we'd stroked the scaly neck of the gigantic 150-year-old tortoise, when our attention was captured by a piercing shriek. Vivien had begun dancing wildly around on the grass, jumping from one foot to the other, spinning in circles, touching her toes and slapping at her legs, emitting a strange rhythmic noise, a cross between a squeal and a roar, like some kind of frantic pagan mating ritual. It was out-of-character as she usually kept a low profile, watching all the time from the background to ensure that everybody was enjoying themselves, and we all stood and stared at her in astonishment as she leapt and bellowed.

Between swipes and curses, she yelled: '*Siafu*! Safari ants!' She had managed to stand in a nest of the awful creatures, and they had got up inside her trousers. Anybody who has had *siafu* going up inside their trousers will tell you that modesty is not an issue, and she was preparing to publicly strip down to her undies. Elephant Man steered her, with her trousers half-way down her legs, into the privacy of a nearby building where she could despatch the ghastly insects. They inflict an incredibly painful bite and have a similar tenacity to a bull terrier; once they have clamped their pincers closed, it's impossible to prise them apart.

Still, they can be useful. Once it has bitten a safari ant would sooner die than let go, so they can be, and have been used as stitches to close a wound. By encouraging the ants to bite each side of the wound and then removing their bodies from their heads, the strong pincers hold the wound closed.

I recalled a gruesome story about a drunken man at a mission who had run amok and been locked in a shed for the night for his own safety. He screamed for several hours, screams that were ignored, put down to his drunkenness. Eventually they stopped. When morning came and the door was opened, all that remained was a skeleton where his flesh had been stripped by the ants. I don't know how true the story is, but from personal experience I can testify that these creatures are ravenous and single-minded, as I found out long ago when on a fishing trip on Mount Kenya. I went behind some bushes to answer a call of nature, discreetly out of sight of the rest of our party and immediately stood on a trail of the ants. They swarmed over my shoes and onto my legs. Their bites feel as if you have been stabbed with red hot needles and injected with acid.

Vivien returned with her clothing in place and a few nasty bites on her legs, and Elephant Man ushered us to meet some Colobus monkeys with their long glossy black and white coats – sadly sought after as tribal costume – that searched our hands for treats with their soft, busy little fingers, and sat upon our heads. Incongruously, there was a white llama grazing on the lawn. It came and gazed into my face with limpid eyes. I was ready to duck if it decided to spit – I've tasted llama spit once before – but it just stared placidly.

Terry and Colobus monkey

Elephant Man explained that the llamas were originally brought to Kenya for use as pack animals for people climbing Mount Kenya. Once they were no longer needed – maybe people discovered that Kenya mules could serve the same purpose? – they were donated to the orphanage where they live in comfortable retirement. Although they looked peculiarly out of place 7,000 miles from home, they thrive in the climate which is similar to their native Andes.

An ancient zebroid, a cross between a horse and a zebra drowsed in the sun, the profile of a horse and the stripes of a zebra indicating its parentage. Nearby were a couple of Africa's second most ferocious animals, responsible for more deaths than any other creature except the mosquito. For the moment they looked as innocent as kittens, as they stood awaiting a delivery of fruit. Although these two were pygmy hippos, they were still a formidable size and equally as dangerous as their full-sized relatives. Their immense jaws were like the buckets of mechanical diggers, gaping wide as whole watermelons were tossed into them. One munch reduced the fruit to a mushy red mess that dribbled out of their rubbery lips. It was like a scene from a horror film.

In a spacious enclosure, an elegant cheetah lay in the shade watching us through lazy eyes. She was so slender and elegant, her coat blending into the dappled light and her expression saying that she knew how beautiful she was, that she was the star of the show. Elephant Man slipped a collar and lead on her, and then opened her enclosure so that we could go and stroke her. She was relaxed and docile, purring with pleasure as she rolled on her back and allowed us to scratch her belly. Unlike the other big cats, lions, tigers and leopards, cheetahs are not aggressive towards humans, and many have been successfully kept as pets particularly in the Middle East where they are used for hunting. They seem to have a natural affinity with man. However, you would not want to make them angry. When Ken crouched down close and pointed his camera at her, she was upright and baring her teeth in a blur of spotted fur.

Now that we had met and admired all the animal residents, Elephant Man began to tell us how he came by his name. We gathered around him in a circle. This is his story in his own words.

James and another ranger, Donald Bunge who is now the Wildlife Manager, were at the bongo enclosure a couple of miles from the orphanage. Bongo are magnificent antelope native to the forests around Mount Kenya. To save them from near extinction, they were being bred in the United States and then brought to Kenya to become acclimatised and prepared to return to their natural wild habitat.

The rangers knew that there were elephants in the

vicinity, but they had no idea that they were about to be attacked by them. The elephants came towards the *boma* – the enclosure – and began breaking it down. As the two rangers tried to move them away back into the forest, a rogue bull elephant appeared between the two men and came running towards James, 'opening his ears and making a lot of noise by trumpeting and throwing water from his mouth.'

As James ran, trying to hide from the mad bull, he tripped on some wood and fell to the ground. The elephant charged, and he thought he would be trampled, but instead the animal knelt down and stabbed him with a tusk. One tusk pierced his back near the ribs. The bull picked him up and tossed him down. Then it knelt down again and thrust its tusk into his abdomen, and threw him on top of a bush. He saw the bull returning and charging towards him where he lay on the bush, and he managed to jump from the bush and hide behind a big tree trunk, holding his stomach in with his hands.

The elephants surrounded him, but he had his radio in his hand and was able to call for help. He spoke to the legendary founder of the Mount Kenya Game Ranch, Don Hunt, who gathered all the rangers, rescued Elephant Man, and took him to hospital in Nanyuki, 35 minutes away. He had sustained four broken ribs and the tusks had pierced his liver, lungs and diaphragm. As he underwent two 6-hour operations and was given 4 pints of blood, his wife and three children cried for 5 days believing it was impossible that he could survive such an attack. But there he was, living proof that he could indeed not only survive but return to work 6 months later.

Pulling open his jacket, he showed us the huge scars on his back and abdomen. He is a slightly-built man, tall but slender, and seeing those scars and having recently been so close to elephants ourselves, it seemed truly miraculous that anybody could recover from such injuries. I don't know how many people have survived being knelt upon and gored by an elephant, but I can't imagine there are very many, which makes James Muraya a remarkable man.

That was 8 years ago. He still suffers from digestive problems and is only able to eat soup and rice, and he has nightmares about elephants. He doesn't like to see them, and who can blame him?

The elephant that had injured him killed two rangers before it was shot.

Before dinner that evening, Terry and I sat and watched the sun go down and the mountain go to sleep for the night, sharing a bottle of Tusker, the iconic Kenyan lager that is exported all over the world and loved by ex-Kenyans.

One of my earliest jobs was at Allsopps Brewery at Ruaraka where the lager was produced. I was the secretary to the Sales Manager, Plant Manager and Chief Brewer. As the brewery was several miles outside Nairobi, my colleague, the Managing Director's secretary and I were chauffeured to and from the brewery every day, which gave my 17-year-old self a sense of great importance. :) We were entitled to a crate of Tusker or Pilsner every week, which was a bonus for my father. I think back to those days rather wistfully, remembering how the men used to bring me half a dozen bars of chocolate every day, competing among themselves to see who could please me most, and I could eat every morsel and still weigh under seven stone.

While we were at Amboseli there were no regulations regarding dress, but a hangover from the old colonial days at Mount Kenya Safari Club is the house rule that gentlemen are required to wear a jacket and long trousers in the dining room in the evening. Unfortunately, one of the members of our party – big Bob whom we have already come to love – turned up in little boy trousers and was sent to his room in disgrace, missing an excellent meal and leaving us all rather subdued.

The next leg of our journey was a relatively short drive. As we would not have to be up at sparrow's crack for our departure, we spent a couple of hours in the bar, sitting in comfort before a flickering log fire and soaking up the atmosphere before retiring to our huge and luxurious room with its en suite marble bathroom spacious enough to dance a polka. While we had been dining, room service had lit a fire in the open fireplace, and the room was deliciously warm with just the faintest welcome scent of wood smoke. It seemed strange that there we were on the equator, with warm, sunny daytime temperatures and yet the nights are really quite cold. We were grateful for the fire. I dozed on and off, watching the embers of the fire twinkling in the dark and trying to find a position where my shoulder didn't hurt.

At hour twelve of the night, I got up and drew back the curtains. Mount Kenya filled the bedroom window in all her early morning splendour, her snowy mantle tinted with the pink and gold of sunrise.

Once again, I'm going into food mode here, please bear with me. I'll try to restrain myself in future but I must share the experience of breakfast at the club, because it really is something quite special, and would make those extravagant Victorian breakfasts once cooked in stately homes look meagre in comparison.

There were four different types of porridge for a start. Yoghurts in myriad flavours. Every kind of fresh fruit imaginable including one I have never seen before, called a thorn melon. One chef cooked pancakes to order. At the juice bar a lady stood ready to produce any juice you asked for from the fresh fruit. Next to her, a chef cooked omelettes to taste. Sausages, bacon, mushrooms, tomatoes, kedgeree, hash browns, rosti, smoothies, bowls of dry cereal, dried fruits, spices, cakes, biscuits, buns, jams, syrups, savoury spreads and cheeses. Coffees, teas, infusions, tisanes. And I counted (just out of interest) 31 different types of breads in various shapes and sizes and flavoured with everything you can think of that could possibly flavour bread. Croissants, doughnuts, bagels, fried bread. I've never seen a spread to match this anywhere in the world.

Congratulating myself for my self-control, I stuck with my usual breakfast of orange juice, coffee and a slice or two of toast and butter. However, satisfying these modest needs turned out to be quite a challenge, as the only thing that staff didn't do (although I'm sure they would have done so if asked) was to make the toast. Guests did that for themselves with an eccentric toaster. At home we like our toast very well done, and I make it in a cast iron frying pan over the gas. We have an electric toaster, but we prefer it cooked that way. It reminds me of being a child and toasting the bread over a coal fire. I can usually create toast without difficulty, but on this occasion I had to admit defeat. Having carefully selected two slices of the grainiest and most fragrant organic bread on offer, I fed them into the toasting machine, which was rather archaic in design and something of a 'character'. You put the slices onto a sloping wire frame, down which they gently slid onto a slow metal conveyor that swallowed them up until they momentarily disappeared. Theoretically they should have emerged golden brown on both sides and swooshed out onto a tray at the bottom, all crispy and hot.

My slices did not emerge. I tried poking and prodding into the bowels of the machine with a knife, without any result other than a minor burn on my hand. After two slices have vanished without trace, a man came over and tilted the machine onto three legs, jamming a teaspoon beneath the fourth leg. 'About time this was replaced,' he said. 'It's been on the way out for years. I'm an old-timer here and used to its funny ways. There you go.' He slipped a couple of slices onto the rack and a minute or so later they arrived on the tray. I don't know where the first two went as they never appeared. As eccentric as it was, the strange machine lent a nice human touch to the otherwise perfection of the dining room.

Then there was the honey. At home we buy from a local producer, and the honey comes in clear plastic jars. At the club it comes directly from the comb, hanging from a stainless steel frame from which it drips in its own sweet time onto a chute from where it slithers seductively into waiting bowls. For all the splendour of that breakfast, it will always be the images of the toast machine and dripping honey that remain most vividly in my mind.

Chapter Thirteen

SPEAK SWAHILI: KIBOKO – HIPPO

When we checked out of the club the next morning, the Receptionist glanced through our passports before handing them back. He was delighted to see that my name is Susan, which is also, he told me, the name of his favourite aunt. With a big laugh, he said that he was adopting me as his *mzungu* aunt.

The bizarre pain in my shoulder continued. It was never there at breakfast and didn't bother me at all during our drives, but as soon as we sat down in the evening, it kicked in and lasted through the night. It was agonising, as if something was eating it from the inside out, and it was getting worse. The tablets from Amboseli had not helped. It passed all understanding. Our next location was the Samburu Game Reserve, in Kenya's desolate north-eastern region, where medical facilities would be extremely limited.

We had medical insurance to cover emergencies, including air evacuation. I didn't think it was likely I would need that, but as we were very close to Nanyuki town, and as we had time to spare Vivien and Kamara took me to the little cottage hospital there. It's an elderly, old-fashioned building, brightly painted and standing in beautiful gardens. Vivien had to use all her powers of persuasion to make the single duty doctor see me – incidentally the same doctor who had operated on Elephant Man after his horrific accident. He was clearly exhausted, overworked, under-staffed, under-funded and extremely irritated, and told me frankly that he had dozens of patients who were critically ill and in need of attention, but he did scribble out a prescription which I took to the hospital dispensary, where a gentle girl meticulously counted out the prescribed number of tablets into a brown paper envelope which she carefully sealed and handed back to me with a shy smile. The total cost for the consultation and tablets was only $10.

Our journey northwards led through the spectacularly fertile and productive landscape of the Meru district, one of Kenya's major wheat-growing areas. A recent Government initiative had made loans to local groups of small farmers to enable them to purchase greenhouses to raise their crops more productively, while large multi-national companies were growing roses and vegetables in huge poly-tunnels for export to Europe. Personally, I think they spoil the beauty of the natural landscape, and I am unashamedly old-fashioned in that I prefer food that is grown close to home with as little man-made interference as possible. However, with its tremendous population explosion Kenya and its people need work and they need commerce, and this is the 21st century's way of optimising production by controlling the environment in which the crops are grown. Dedan was critical, saying that the commercial businesses are monopolising the precious water from Mount Kenya to the detriment of small independent farmers and families.

As we drove, he explained how M-Pesa works and I learned what a brilliantly successful and simple system it is, a great Kenyan success story and the world's largest mobile money market. There are around 40,000 M-Pesa agents around the country, and even in the most remote areas where there is nothing more than a 'general store' shack the M-Pesa signs can be found. A person pays cash into their account at any one of those agents and can then use their mobile phone to pay their bills and transfer money to friends and family who can collect the cash from their nearest M-Pesa agent.

As soon as they have clicked the OK button to confirm the transfer, the recipient's phone pings to tell them they have received funds. They don't need bank accounts because they can manage all their financial affairs through their mobile phones, and they don't need expensive smart phones, either, because M-Pesa does not use the internet, it works through the excellent mobile phone network. I don't have accurate figures, but am told that something like 90% of Kenyans now have a mobile phone. Before M-Pesa the only way for people to send money long distances was by giving cash to somebody to deliver, and trusting that they would do so, or making bank transfers for those who actually had a bank account. Now people don't need to risk carrying large amounts of cash, and can do everything from paying their bus fares, making their loan repayments, purchasing goods online and carrying out business transactions. For those living in remote rural areas it has revolutionised their lives.

I wish we had something similar in France but it wouldn't work that well for us, as to get a signal at home we have to roam around the garden waving the mobile phone in the air. There are times when we need to receive a text message containing a code for some Internet transaction, but by the time we manage to get a signal and find the code, the page has often expired. Kenya's mobile network is far better.

We stopped at a curio shop for an opportunity to use the bathroom. As I had no need, I sat outside talking to some of the men who worked there in the shop. With their income depending upon sales from the shop's goods, I didn't want to give them false hope, because I was definitely not intending to buy anything. They were interested to learn we live in France, and like most Kenyans they were football fans and wanted to know if we supported Paris St Germain. Not being fans, that was the only team I'd heard of, so I said yes anyway. :)

All the while that we were talking, their eyes were alert for new tourist arrivals. When a minibus pulled into the car park one of the older men murmured urgently to a youngster, who swiftly caught the new arrivals as they disembarked. With the tourist industry hit hard by recent negative media attention, people whose livelihood depended on tourism for their daily bread could not afford to let a crumb slip through their fingers.

As we continued northwards, the luxuriant countryside dwindled away to a harsh, barren landscape of blazing white dust, sand, rocks and scrubby thorn trees. If ever there was an example of optimism over reality, it must surely be the Isiolo Lawn Tennis Association, whose office on the outskirts of the town bears the slogan 'Dream of Excellence'. The association was formed in 2014 with the noble aim of introducing and developing lawn tennis recreational facilities in Isiolo County, to promote the growth of tennis as a sport to the highest level, as well as initiating schools tennis programmes in the county. Their mission is to mobilise local people to participate in sports for recreation, career development and for good health. It is an example of the indomitable spirit of the Kenyan people. They were not deterred from their dream of grass tennis courts despite the fact that there is not a single blade of greenery for as far as the eye can see. Whether they will flourish or wither away, who could tell, but they had support from the very top of the tennis tree – we had missed Roger Federer's visit to the club by three weeks.

At Isiolo, gateway to Kenya's Northern Frontier District, we stopped in a dusty street reminiscent of a film set from the Wild West, nothing more than a ragged collection of run-down buildings where not even tumbleweed tumbled. It is home to a large Somali community, handsome people who carry themselves proudly, but they were poorly dressed and emanated a quiet air of resignation and hopelessness. They stood watching us through narrowed eyes. 'Put your cameras away,' Vivien hissed. 'Hide them.'

I asked Dedan why the people objected to being

photographed, and he replied that they believe people take their photos and sell them to magazines for a lot of money, but they don't get paid anything. I could see their point. If I was as impoverished as they are, I'd probably resent people profiting from broadcasting it.

Vivien climbed out and asked – well, ordered, she can be a bossy little person – all of us to stay in our vehicles and to keep the doors and windows locked. Kamara joined her as they vanished into a crowd of jostling, shouting people. We all sat obediently locked into the Land Cruisers and were instantly surrounded by vendors thrusting sunglasses, hats, jewellery, carvings, fruit and vegetables and catapults at the windows. They tapped on the glass, called out and waved their goods around, and we smiled and waved back, shaking our heads. They shouted louder and tapped harder, and we shook our heads more vigorously and waved faster and smiled more.

After ten minutes, Kamara came back to say through a tiny gap Dedan opened in the window, that Vivien had asked a Somali lady who sold bananas to put five in each vehicle – a snack to add to our biscuits and sweeties for the rest of the drive. We didn't actually need bananas, having breakfasted like kings and with lunch awaiting us, but Vivien always tried to help everybody, including people who sold bananas and who badly needed money.

A tiny Somali lady arrived, bent over and dwarfed by a load of bananas almost as big as her. She shouted that she had been told to give five bananas to each vehicle, so we opened the door and in they came. Five of them. Ten. Fifteen. Twenty. An almighty, overwhelming torrent of bananas. We tried to push the surplus out, but she kept pushing them back in until they were up to our knees. There were four of us, and she was so small, but her determination was stronger than our combined force. While our attention had been on the banana bonanza and our struggle to close the door against it, somebody had forced open one of the windows on the other side of the vehicle, and a young man was waving some beaded jewellery in my face.

'No, thank you,' I said.

'We need money,' he replied. 'We don't beg and we don't steal. Do you know how long it takes to make these beautiful things for you? How hard we have worked, just to make a few shillings? Don't you want to help us to live?' I did. Of course I did.

He offered me six bracelets – which are all too small to fit over my large hands – for $10, and accepted my offer of $8. I handed him a $10 note.

'What else would you like?' he asked.

'That's all I want today, thanks. Just the change, please.'

'I don't have any change. But I'll give you two necklaces. Choose which ones you would like.' He shoved a bundle of beaded necklaces through the window which he kept wedged open with a determined elbow.

How can I refuse a couple of dollars for all the materials and time that have gone into making these articles?

I picked two and put them in my bag with the shell necklace I had bought from the silver-tongued devil on our way back from Amboseli. So I now had three necklaces, and six bracelets that didn't fit.

Most of the vendors were Somali ladies, narrow-featured, elegant in head scarves and colourful shabby robes. One of them engaged Michael in conversation.

'Would you like to meet for a drink?' she asked.

'Not now. Maybe when we come back,' he replied, laughing.

'I will give you my phone number,' she said, scribbling something on a piece of paper, which Michael accepted politely.

Vivien finally returned to the vehicle surrounded by half a dozen traders all speaking urgently. They knew her well, and gave her quantities of goods to sell for them. Her bag bulged with intricate metalwork bracelets and beautiful amber necklaces. She would get a very good price for them in the United States, and send the money to the traders.

'What on earth are all these bananas doing?' she shouted when she saw us peering over the top of them. We explained about the banana lady's persistence, and as we spoke we could see her bearing down upon us with a fresh load.

'Drive, Dedan,' Vivien said.

As he led our convoy out of town, a police vehicle pulled in ahead of us, and another behind. I could hear Vivien speaking to Dedan in Swahili. I realised that she did not want us to know what she was saying, but I could still remember sufficient Swahili to understand that there may be a problem ahead. I asked her in Swahili what was happening.

'There are reports of a *fitina* up ahead between the Samburu and Turkana,' she said. 'So the police are giving us an armed escort to make sure we aren't held up.'

The northern frontier is a volatile area that has been a regular battleground for inter-tribal fights over cattle as far back as anybody can remember, as well as religious differences between the Christians and the predominantly Muslim Somalis. Because of this there is a generally uneasy atmosphere among the people living here, but these problems are between the local people and not aimed at tourists. However, as the safety and security of tourists is paramount the police were there to guarantee our safe passage.

A few miles down the stony road, we came across a piece of wood halfway across the road acting as a barrier to traffic, and half a dozen men standing around chatting and laughing, armed with sticks. The police spoke to them briefly and then turned around, saluting us as they headed back to town. The stickmen moved the piece of wood from the road, waving and smiling as we passed. All our guides were from the

Kikuyu tribe, and the Samburu stickmen had no quarrel with anybody except their historic enemy, the Turkana. Cattle rustling is an age-old occupation, fuelled by the increasing demand for cheap meat. We *mzungu* travellers had nothing to fear, but if they caught up with the rustlers, justice would be swift and brutal.

Chapter Fourteen

SPEAK SWAHILI: MOJA, MBILI, TATU – ONE, TWO, THREE

The landscape here was so inhospitable, yet at the same time beautiful with its clear bright light, the cloudless blue of the sky and the absence of any buildings. Along the glaring white dust of the road for mile after mile beneath a blazing sun, men were hacking at the ground with pick axes, digging a trench to house electrical cables for communications. The soil was concrete-hard, just dust and rocks, back-breaking work for men who would earn next to nothing but were swinging their picks energetically. In a country where there is high unemployment, any work is welcome.

Our route passed the Lewa Wildlife Conservancy, where Prince William proposed to Kate Middleton, taking the first steps towards creating the next generation of the British monarchy.

Half an hour later, we were at Archers Post, a small straggly settlement which, if you pinpoint it on a map of Kenya, is almost exactly at the centre. (Incidentally, I compared the outline of Kenya with the outline of France – they are both hexagonal and remarkably similar.)

We arrived in time for lunch at Samburu Game Lodge, which sits on the banks of the Uaso Nyiro river which was alarmingly shallow, nothing more than a wide gulley with a few puddles that glistened like broken shards of mirror in the red sand. The rains weren't due for another two months.

Our accommodation was in timber-clad cottages with traditional *makuti* roofs made from the dried leaves of the coconut palm. Rustic on the outside to blend in with the environment, inside the rooms were sunny and spacious, elegantly furnished and decorated in Maasai/Samburu style. As the porters carried our bags along the pathway, eyes watched every move we made as the ubiquitous baboons sloped around in the bushes, on the roofs and up the trees. Despite their fearsome teeth and sharp eyes they were not aggressive, and moved aside politely as we passed.

Lunching in the open dining room, 50 yards away across the riverbed, I saw for the first time several beisa oryx grazing beside a small herd of elephants. They are hefty, striking antelope with very long, thin pointed horns and coats of a creamy-grey colour that looked almost lavender in the right light.

Spear-wielding Samburu men in their traditional costumes patrolled the grounds of the lodge. We were standing on a terrace just below the dining room and I asked one of them how close the wild animals came.

'Sometimes they can come very close,' he replied. 'Last night an elephant was standing here. It left its dung there.' He pointed with his spear to a slightly darkened patch a couple of feet away with a few shreds of grass still stuck to it. On the way back to our bungalow we walked towards the river bank, and as we rounded the corner almost walked into a heap of elephant dung, like a pile of cannon balls. Wisps of steam rose from it and it gave off a surprisingly mild almost sweet smell, like grass mowings that had been in the sun. Beside it were great footprints, with trickles of sand still tumbling into the depressions they had made. Stacey and Mike had an elephant right outside their bungalow. Despite the very close proximity of all these wild creatures there was no sense of danger, but rather a sense of being completely at peace and in harmony with nature.

There was a display of traditional dancing taking place at the swimming pool, but we decided instead to have a walk around the grounds, where we came upon a mass of dwarf mongooses playing. Cute little creatures whose diet consists mainly of insects, small amphibians and snakes, they make a funny high-pitched noise called giggling while they are mating. That could be off-putting. They were all over the place; we counted thirty scampering through the grass, racing around the bases of trees and jumping out and pouncing on each other like schoolboys in a playground. The plural is mongooses, not mongeese and collectively they are called a business. Don't ask me why. I have no idea. Who makes up these collective nouns?

Our first sighting on the afternoon drive was a couple of sturdy waterbuck, who have always been one of my favourite antelope. I was a bit surprised to see them in this parched place because unlike many other antelope species they do not thrive in dry conditions, and are water-dependent, hence their name. I hoped it would rain soon.

This was the furthest north I had ever been in Kenya, and it was the first time I had seen the rare and beautiful reticulated giraffe. They have distinctly different markings from their Maasai cousins, far more geometrical and neater, as if they have taken greater care when painting their pattern. I loved their elegant, slow-motion lollop, their necks swaying gently as they sashayed across the ground with lazy strides, swinging those long, long legs like pendulums.

'Have you considered how a giraffe drinks?' Dedan asked. I must admit this is not something that had previously preoccupied me, but when I considered it I could see that it could pose a problem, bending the head all that way down to ground level and drawing water up such a long neck. A giraffe's heart has to be very strong to pump blood up to the brain, so if the neck is down and the heart is working hard, surely all the blood will go into its head? What does it do – stop its heart? No. Firstly, it must bend and splay apart its forelegs to lower its body, because otherwise it can't reach the ground with its mouth, which is possibly an engineering design fault? However, the designers redeem themselves by equipping the giraffe's neck with a series of non-return valves to control the flow of blood. Isn't nature wonderful?

Dedan mentioned that the collective name for a group of giraffe is a tower, and the 'horns' on its head are called ossicones, which are comprised of cartilage that hardens into bone as the animal grows into adulthood. Although giraffe are herbivores, they are frequently seen chewing bones to obtain the large amounts of calcium needed to support their long bones. They also act as pollinators, carrying pollen from one tree to another. How much you can learn in just a couple of minutes.

Our guides all carried mobile phones so they could alert each other to what was happening where, so when Dedan took a call from Steve and made a sudden U-turn we knew we were going to see something special. We drove to a rocky outcrop topped by small plateau covered with thorny scrub where a couple of vehicles were parked up but there was nothing to see. When asked what we were looking for, Dedan suggested that we should sit quietly and wait, which we did for several minutes. There was a slight movement among the low branches, and then we saw her, a majestic leopard, her spotted coat providing perfect camouflage as she stalked through the bushes before coming into full view. With a disdainful glance towards the vehicles, she climbed onto the plateau and sat gazing out onto the plains as if she was searching for something. After no more than a minute, she jumped down and vanished instantly back into the bushes. The recent negative publicity regarding travel to Kenya had drastically affected the tourist industry, and while this has had a devastating effect on all those who depend upon it for their living, it did mean that traffic in the parks was sparse, which was better for the animals and better for us.

Later, we returned to the rock to see if she was still there, but there was no sign. Unlike lions and cheetah who were always easily visible and seemingly comfortable in the presence of humans, the leopards were elusive and secretive.

As we continued our drive through the reserve we met a herd of elephants, among them a mature female with an infant. Unusually, the adult had no tusks at all. Studies over the last few decades have found that in an increasing percentage of elephants their tusks are getting smaller and in some cases vanishing completely. Without tusks they have no value to the poachers who are decimating elephants worldwide to supply man's greed for ivory. The more that can reach adulthood without growing tusks the better chance the species has for survival, and although their tusks serve as valuable tools for foraging, they can learn to adapt without them by using their feet and trunks. Whether this is due to a natural evolutionary process, or ingenious genetic engineering by the elephants I don't know, but it can only be a good thing if it protects them.

If Dedan hadn't mentioned it I doubt we would have noticed that many of the elephants show greater signs of wear to one tusk than the other, because just as humans are left- or right-handed, so elephants favour one tusk more than the other. Once we knew, we could see this quite clearly as they were only a couple of yards from our vehicle. By then we were becoming accustomed to seeing elephants at close quarters, but each time there was the same sense of awe, the magic of being close to these powerful gentle giants, especially watching the tender way the whole herd protected their young.

Heading back to the lodge before the evening curfew, we stopped to admire a lone lion dozing in a patch of shade on the bank of the river, watching with mild interest a dozen giraffe – a tower, as Dedan reminded us – a hundred yards away, either unaware or unconcerned by the presence of the big cat. Close by, a family of elephants on the river bed were scraping at the drying sand. Since we arrived, the puddles had shrunk further.

In the dining room that evening, there was a pretty, feline-looking creature with large ears and eyes, wearing a silver coat spotted with black splodges. It was quite at home running along the low stone wall and jumping onto tables. I thought it was either a serval, a civet or a genet, my knowledge of them being minimal.

'Does anybody know what this is?' I asked.

'It's called Janet,' said Deb. 'The waitress told me.'

That answered my question. Somebody offered Janet the genet a piece of meat which she swiped and swallowed in one swift movement. She went quickly from table to table around the room, stopping briefly to see who would feed her. After a while she came back to the wall and sat watching us. I reached out towards her, and in a blur of black, silver and pink tongue she sank her sharp little teeth into my hand. Not deeply; I think she thought I was offering her something. There was no malice involved, just a misunderstanding, but I wouldn't be putting my fingers near her face again.

One of the armed watchmen walked us back to our bungalow by torchlight. I was wondering if it was really necessary, or a little bit of theatre put on for tourists, and if there were likely to be any wild animals so close to us, when we passed within touching distance of two kudu grazing on the lawn, and I remembered the steaming heap of elephant dung we had seen earlier. We stood outside for a few minutes listening to the sounds of the night – snorts, chewing, squeaks and rustles, the chirping of crickets and rustling leaves. In the distance, something was barking. And the night air was soft and comforting.

Chapter Fifteen

SPEAK SWAHILI: NNE, TANO, SITA – FOUR, FIVE, SIX

It was only when we woke just before daybreak that I realised my shoulder had stopped hurting and I'd slept for ten hours. Hooray!

Vivien arranged that each day we shared the vehicles with different people and different guides to drive us, so that we all had a chance to get to know each other. On our second day in Samburu our guide was David, a passionate ecologist whose greatest love apart from his family is the black rhino. Nearly always smiling, with his sunglasses tilted back on his head, he had a powerful muscular body that you thought would stand him in good stead versus a rhino. He was always beautifully dressed, his trousers held up by one of the gorgeous beaded belts I hankered after. As we drove onto the plains, the sun burst up into the horizon. It would make a stunning photo so we asked David if he would stop, and he said yes but kept driving so we thought he had misunderstood, when after a couple of hundred yards he pulled over and turned the vehicle, perfectly positioned so that a solitary acacia tree stood silhouetted against the sunrise.

'Now you have the best angle,' he said. 'That is the shot you want.' Of course, he was quite right. It was the iconic Kenyan scene.

We drove back to the rocky place where we had seen the leopard the previous day. She was there again but seemed a little agitated, walking backwards and forwards on the plateau of rocks, raising her head and mewing. An answering mew came from our right. On the other side of the track, a cub appeared some distance away, timidly peeping through a bush. The mother called to it again, and the cub advanced, and then jumped back. It was clearly nervous of the half a dozen parked vehicles blocking its route to its mother. The drivers backed away to allow it more space. There are strict regulations regarding treatment of the wild animals who have right of way at all times, and it is forbidden to harass them in any way. The cub crept forward, ducked back, came a few steps closer. All the while the two animals were calling to each other. Suddenly, the cub made a dash past the vehicles to its mother, and the two of them vanished in a blink, as if they were never there. I couldn't help smiling to myself as I watched a photographer in another vehicle – not one of our group. He had a massive lens on his camera, and in his hurry to turn and catch the cub running, he cracked another passenger on the head.

A couple of miles and five minutes later we met a cheetah who unlike the shy leopard was completely comfortable in our presence. She was watching a couple of tiny dik dik antelope about twenty yards away, and began to walk stealthily towards them; but they had already seen or scented her and took off into the distance, and she seemed to shrug before lying down, as if she wasn't that interested any way.

'They were too far away,' David said. 'Cheetah can run very fast, but only for a short distance. If she doesn't catch them quickly, her oxygen will run out. She knew that.'

I was pleased. She didn't look hungry. That was just a half-hearted chase.

The plains are dotted with termite mounds – also called ant hills – deep red towering chimneys contrasting with the golden grass and dust. David knows a lot about termite hills and the life inside them. The termite community is a collective, able to construct and maintain the huge structure by the combined efforts of its tiny residents. The workers collect dry grass and decaying wood that they take into the nest and cultivate to grow fungus to feed themselves. The height of a hill is an indication of the depth, as the visible mound represents the quantity of soil the insects have had to move to create the underground chambers where they live and work, and feed the queen. She is a bloated lump whose only purpose is to produce eggs – up to 30,000 per day, which are fertilised by her diminutive king. Termite queens can live for up to twenty years, but once they stop churning out baby termites they have outlived their usefulness and the workers who have pampered them during their productive years will eat them. Alive. When she dies, the whole colony will die.

The hard-working little termites perform a useful task in clearing and composting dead wood and vegetation, and feeding the digested organic waste back into the soil. Their towering nests make scratching posts for large animals, and useful vantage points for scanning the landscape for food or predators. David pointed to a mound next to us. You can tell it's abandoned, he said, because there are plants growing on it.

'How do you guides know so much about everything?' somebody asked.

'We are always learning from what we see with our own eyes, what others teach us, and from studying. That is our job, to know about the land and the wildlife. You are not just coming to see things, you are coming to learn and be amazed at how nature works. We are always learning. In the evenings when I am relaxing, I spend a lot of time reading scientific articles and watching videos on the internet with my iPad,' he said. 'We can never learn too much.'

Back at the lodge, when I was sorting out my things (actually still desperately hunting to see if I had tucked my bras into some pocket that I've overlooked – unfortunately I hadn't), I found at the bottom of my backpack a Camembert cheese left over from our journey. Even though it is best eaten when extremely ripe, this one had really gone too far; the stench was overpowering, so I put it outside under a tree to see whether anything would eat it.

The baboons that lived around the grounds came to investigate. Each one cautiously approached, sniffed, prodded, and then ran away as fast as it could. I sat watching them, wondering if any would actually taste it. One by one they came, all watching each other, and all reacting with the same disgust. After two days, it still lay untouched; even the insects and birds weren't interested in excessively ripe Camembert.

Walking towards the dining room for lunch, we heard a frightful noise of screaming coming from the riverbed below the path. When Ken joined us, he said that there had been a vicious fight between two baboon troops and a baby had been killed. The mother was clutching it, although it was clear that the little creature was quite dead. Typically, she would continue carrying her baby for many days. I was glad we hadn't witnessed that, but I still felt so sad that a small life had been lost and a mother left mourning.

Janet the genet was hanging around our table. She was such a pretty animal and looked so innocent that I would have liked to invite her onto my lap and stroke her, but with my hand still stinging from her previous attention, I resisted the urge.

Gerenuk are the most graceful of all the antelope, at least I think so. They are golden red in colour, with huge eyes and ears, and the inside of their ears carries a large distinct black pattern, like a leaf. Like ballerinas with their long slender necks and pencil-thin limbs, they stand on their back legs to browse on leaves beyond the reach of other herbivores, and from which they can extract sufficient moisture to last them for a long time. On our drive that afternoon, we passed a couple in their characteristic pose, nibbling from a rare tree covered in foliage. The male's profile was a series of curves, from his magnificent S-shaped horns, down his arched neck and back, around his rump and down to his tail that was turned up at the tip and ended in a little black tassel.

Never knowing what we would find around the next corner made every moment of our day exciting and I was always prepared for the unexpected, but not for the strange sight that shortly appeared from a moving cloud that was coming towards us. Out of the swirling dust at a height of about 6 feet, emerged a long rounded nose topped with two tiny ears. It was followed by a long neck and a hump. If you are a Star Wars aficionado, think eopie.

The dust cleared and revealed a herd of camels moving on their fat, padded feet across the stony ground, all glossy with bulging bellies and the perpetually disdainful expression common to their species. The adults were cream-coloured with sparse hair, the youngsters reddish brown and rather woolly. Following them, waving a long stick, was a small man wearing a pinstriped jacket with three buttons on the cuffs, a pair of grey trousers with a knife-edge crease down the front, what looked like an ancient aviator's canvas helmet, chewing a twig and carrying a large plastic bottle. He marched up to us and shouted out in English: 'Fire picture' – his way of saying 'Take a photo,' which we all did. In payment he asked for a bottle of chilled mineral water. 'And biscuit!' he yelled. We gave him a handful of ginger biscuits that he stuffed in his pinstriped pocket before waving his stick and driving his herd away.

He was a Boran tribesman, David told us, pastoralists who have exchanged their beloved cattle for camels, which they refer to as 'the long-necked things'. The long-necked things are able to thrive in barren, waterless areas where cattle can not, and are a source of meat and nutritious milk that has the benefit of staying fresh longer than cows' milk. While the camels had been standing around close to us we could see how well-adapted they are for living in the desert. Their very small ears are lined with thick hair to keep out sand, thick woolly eyebrows act as sunshades, long eyelashes protect their eyes, and their slitty nostrils can seal to stop sand blowing up their noses. Not entirely beautiful, but absolutely practical.

On the move again, David pulled up and parked facing a prickly little bush where a turkey-sized, long-legged speckled bird with a rusty-coloured pompom on its head and rather crazed expression was hopping around, stamping and jabbing beneath the bush. It prowled around attacking from all sides, and after ten minutes emerged with something hanging from its mouth. As it strode towards a bush to our left, we noticed for the first time a female crouching there, all but hidden in the undergrowth. The birds were a little too far away for me to see exactly what it had caught, but afterwards, when I enlarged the photo, I could see a small snake that had wrapped itself around the bird's beak in a futile effort to escape its destiny as a courtship gift.

'What is that bird?' somebody asked.

David coughed politely.

'I don't like saying the name of this bird,' he said. 'It is a very rude word.'

'How do you mean?'

'Well, it's a bustard, a buff crested bustard. Excuse me.'

We explained the subtle difference in spelling and pronunciation between a bustard and a bastard, and put his mind at rest. I remember they were a common sight in Machakos; we called them korhaan.

A Somali ostrich sprinted across the road just ahead of us, with its distinctive blue neck and legs. It's only when you get near to an ostrich that you appreciate what enormous birds they are. Their plumage is quite fluffy, and they have the most beautiful big eyes fringed with long lashes, and lethal toenails reminiscent of a velociraptor. Like so many other species, their status is listed as 'vulnerable' by conservation organisations as their habitat diminishes and they are hunted for their feathers, leather and eggs.

We met up with the rest of our group beside a thorn tree on a slight hill, where we got out to inspect a bleached elephant skull. Inside, the texture is like honeycomb, a network of tunnels that act as an amplifier for communication, and reduce the weight of the great head. Nature's engineering never fails to impress.

The elephant, leopard, lion, buffalo and rhino are the so-called Big Five, the animals that game hunters regarded as the most dangerous, elusive and difficult to track and the most prized to kill, and they are still the five animals that the majority of tourists most want to see, which tends to relegate all the other creatures to the second division as if they are of lesser interest, yet I find them all equally fascinating, with their own unique beauty. There is also a Little Five.

The elephant's miniature version is the tiny elephant shrew which gets its name from the elongated nose that looks like an elephant's trunk.

Leopard tortoises don't share the leopard's speed, nor its carnivorous diet, but are so called because of the rosette pattern on their shell that is similar to the leopard's markings.

The ant lion is the larval stage of a winged insect. It earns its name from its predatory hunting behaviour. A ferocious little creature, it lurks in craters in the sand waiting for unwary small insects to venture too close. A trickle of sand into the crater alerts the ant lion, which springs out like a jet-propelled jack-in-the-box and grabs the hapless creature. I remember trying to lure these little monsters from their hiding place by tickling the sand with a blade of grass, but they did not seem interested in a vegetarian diet and I never did manage to catch one.

Buffalo birds – their correct name is buffalo weaver – bear no resemblance to a buffalo either in appearance or behaviour. They generally hang around where buffalo graze, feeding on the insects disturbed by the animals.

Anybody who has seen a rhinoceros beetle would instantly recognise where it gets its name from – the huge 'horn' on the front of its head.

We moved on to discussing the Ugly Five: the warthog, the hyena, the marabou stork, wildebeeste and vulture. While the marabou is seriously challenged in the good looks department and it would be difficult to describe it as 'beautiful' it does have a regal dignity shared by the vultures, who are magnificent in flight and when they spread their wings to their full extent. Personally I find the hyena with its golden spotted coat, the warthog with its barrel belly and tail held vertically like an aerial both attractive, and as for the gnu – or wildebeeste to give them their alternative name, I've already said that they are one of my favourite animals. With

95

their metallic, silvery-grey coats, their sleek bodies, long wise heads and the white beards that catch the sun, their easy canter or impetuous gallop and buck, I cannot see any ugliness. As babies their little horns stick up like a devil's, and as they mature they spread out and curve up and inwards in an elegant sweep. As they say, beauty is in the eye of the beholder, and this beholder finds them beautiful.

The only creature I find to be truly ugly both in looks and behaviour is the crocodile. They just aren't beautiful, no matter which way you look at them. Nope.

Birdlife abounds in the area, and David pointed out a tawny eagle scanning the plains from high up in an acacia tree. Nearby, a dark chanting goshawk was also on look-out, and a few minutes later we met a flock of colourful vulturine guineafowl with their striking neon blue chest and neck feathers, complemented by black and white striped and spotted wings and tail, and ruby red eyes. To top it all, they wear a brown woolly neck warmer. This exotic plumage draws attention away from the fact that they don't have the prettiest faces. This was the first time I had really taken an interest in birds, having always been more of a fur than feather fan. I was starting to appreciate their beauty and diversity, which was entirely due to the enthusiasm and knowledge of our guides.

Chapter Sixteen

SPEAK SWAHILI: SABA, NANE, TISA, KUMI – SEVEN, EIGHT, NINE, TEN

So many images stick in my mind from our trip. Being within touching distance of elephants and later standing amongst the orphans, close enough to lions to smell them and count their whiskers, the great migration which we would witness later on, and on the seventh day of our visit we watched a scene that entranced me.

David was our guide again, and we were sharing the vehicle with ridiculously handsome Tom and his vivacious wife Peggy, a self-confessed 'boat-rocker' from California. I never saw either of them without a smile on their faces.

As we drove out from the lodge at dawn, a message came through to say there was a cheetah with a kill. By the time we arrived, the cheetah had already eaten her fill and was strolling away with a bulging belly, abandoning the remains of her meal to a pair of silver-backed jackals – elegant, light-footed little animals, fox-like, bright-eyed and bushy-tailed.

They trotted over to the carcass, but as they began to dine, two Ruppell's griffon vultures landed nearby with a thump, and bounced towards them. Huge birds weighing twenty pounds, with wingspan over eight feet and standing three feet tall, they were intent on gatecrashing the feast. However, the jackals were not willing to share, and neither were they going to be intimidated despite the size of their uninvited guests. While one ate, the other kept the two birds away. Pound for pound they were reasonably well-matched, but the single jackal was outnumbered two to one, relying on speed, flexibility and courage to chase away the vultures with their lethal talons and hooked beaks. The jackal twisted and turned as the two birds tried to out-flank it to reach the food.

Like autumn leaves in an updraught, high in the sky dark shapes whirled as more vultures spiralled to the ground and hopped over to join the party. Within a couple of minutes, there were eighteen of them, all stalking towards and around the jackals and their meal. Some crouched low, their necks extended threateningly, while others waddled around and stood peering at the action, as if they were awaiting their turn to have a go. The feisty little animals took turns to keep charging at them and chasing them away while its mate ate.

A bolder bird stretched out its wings and lunged, darting between them to grab the carcass and trying to carry it away, but the jackals fought back, both of them leaping at the bird and tugging back their prize.

It was not only we humans who were witnessing this battle. A few meters away, a lone Grévy's zebra stood watching intently, as if it wanted to remember every detail.

An enormous vulture swooped down, wings pinned back, talons and beak thrust forward in a classic attack posture, and one of the jackals leapt up at it. Another bird dive bombed it from behind, huge yellow beak agape, and the jackal swung around to face it. Every few minutes or so there seemed to be a truce, when the birds settled down and stood idly while the jackals ate undisturbed.

By now there were forty birds, a mixture of adults and smaller, daintier juveniles – if a vulture can be regarded as dainty – that lacked the audacity of the adults. Every so often, a few birds surged forward in a group and made a concerted dive at the carcass. The jackals continued fighting the enemy on the land and in the air, and if there had been a beach they would certainly have fought them there too. They were never going to surrender.

Later, from the EXIF (the information that the camera

records for each image) on my photos I saw that this David and Goliath battle had lasted for 26 minutes, until the jackals had dragged away the major part of the carcass, and the vultures fell upon what was left, fighting amongst themselves in a cloud of dust and melee of wings.

Calling somebody a jackal is regarded as a derogatory term. I don't know why. Watching these two little characters defending their property against heavy odds, and selflessly protecting each other so they each eat, I thought them heroic and really quite charming.

We saw several lions later that morning. A couple of young lionesses slept beside each other in the shade of a leafy green shrub, and a little further on, a male padded along leaving great pug marks in the sandy soil. We were within just a few feet of these animals, close enough to count the individual hairs of their coats, see the size of their teeth and paws and the great muscles of their shoulders and haunches.

Chapter Seventeen

SPEAK SWAHILI: JANA – YESTERDAY

At the river, only two slender fingers of water remained in the centre; on each side, the sand was still dark where the water level had been only a few hours before. Two men were digging in the sand, building a channel. It looked as if they were trying to create a pool for the dwindling water. It was an ominous sign, as one adult elephant alone drinks ninety gallons of water a day. David said that during the last severe drought, water had been shipped in for the 'big' game, but the rest had to fend for themselves.

During the droughts, tens of thousands of antelope die. The following year the herds breed, the rains come, the herds grow in number and flourish until the next drought. It's the harsh cycle of life in Africa.

A call came through saying there were lions heading our way, and David switched off the engine while we waited. He asked if in Europe and the United States we have a dowry system. We said no, although Tom and Peggy joked about big diamond rings and mortgages. In Kenya, the dowry still exists and is an important part of Kenyan culture, David told us, although it is no longer paid in goats and cattle, because the value of a bride is so high that the number of animals would be ridiculous. Instead, a symbolic token payment is made, and the full amount takes the form of a lifetime debt that will never end. We asked what token dowry he had paid for his wife.

A large and a small jar of honey, a blanket for her mother, and a coat for her father. The practical use for the coat and blanket are obvious, and the honey is used to brew beer, similar to the mead that dates back to Roman times.

After sitting chatting about cultural differences for a while, our patience was rewarded and we saw a lioness on the far river bank, with the body of an oryx she had killed and was guarding without making any attempt to eat it. Five minutes later, a male lion arrived, and after a few mouthfuls grabbed the carcass and started heaving it towards the bushes. An adult oryx weighs over 400 pounds. As the lion tugged on it, the lioness decided to sit upon it, adding her 250 pounds to the weight. She sat there like a princess on her throne, while the male kept on hauling, stopping every minute or so, and then getting a fresh grip, digging in his heels, and inch by inch moving back into the bushes, showing no sign of being exasperated by the female's thoughtless behaviour. She looked as if she was thinking: 'I caught it, the rest is up to you'.

As the lions vanished, a couple of dik dik appeared in a clearing near us, their enormous eyes fringed with long thick lashes, reminiscent of those drawings of soulful children hugging similarly soulful puppies. Such delicate little animals, not much over a foot in height and so pretty, with elongated, prehensile noses ending in nostrils that look like twin exhaust pipes. They use them to regulate their temperature, and as a musical instrument to whistle an alarm signal when they sense danger. Dik dik can run at over 25 miles an hour, but when they sense danger they tend to hide rather than run, and their preferred habitat is among leafy vegetation where they can tuck themselves away out of sight.

The male has two endearing little horns, and they both sport a jaunty quiff of hair between the ears. David pointed out a prominent black patch with a hole in it beneath their eyes, which is a gland which when they rub it against twigs releases a substance that they use to mark their territory. He climbed out of the vehicle and broke off a thorn from a bush, showing us the black sticky wax on the tip that the dik dik had excreted from the gland. I can't say I'd like to have to stick thorns so close to my eyes.

Our next sighting was the Grévy's zebra, larger than the plains zebra and with narrower stripes which end above its white belly. In the 1970s, there were 15,000 in the wild. Now there are less than 3,000. The rate at which African wildlife is diminishing is alarming and tragic. Who could have imagined that an animal once as abundant as the zebra would be in danger of extinction? No longer just hunted by predators for food, but by humans for trophies, and now losing their habitat and grazing to domestic cattle as humans encroach into the reserves.

Each individual zebra has a unique stripe pattern in the same way as human fingerprints. In the long grass, those stripes camouflage them, and when the herd grazes close together all their patterns merge, creating one confusing amorphous mass to confound predators. The stallions can be distinguished from the mares with their sharper, darker and more clearly defined stripes, whilst the foals were reddish brown with fluffy coats.

When I was a teenager, there was a 'tame' zebra at the Outspan Hotel in Nyeri, and somewhere there's a photo of me sitting on it. I have seen old photos of them pulling carriages, and at the beginning of the 20th century Kenya's first private medical practitioner, a Goan gentleman named Dr Rosendo Ribeiro did his patient rounds in Nairobi riding a tame zebra. However, they don't share the biddable temperament of horses, they are difficult to tame and unpredictable, and in the long run, better suited and happier being left to roam the grasslands as the wild animals they were designed to be.

That afternoon we went on an organised visit to a traditional Samburu village – a *manyatta*. We were greeted by Gabriel, a Samburu elder who like almost all the Kenyans working in the tourist industry spoke beautiful English.

Adorned with several beaded necklaces and bracelets, he was slender, fit and handsome, with a shaved head and a gap in his teeth. He wore a *kikoi* in vibrant turquoise and orange, and those wonderful, durable sandals made from old car tyres that they call '*akala*'. His companion was a little on the plump side but dressed in the same fashion. The two men led us down a very hot dusty path to where a group of ladies were waiting, dressed in bright yellow and red *kikois* fastened over one shoulder to form dresses, all wearing beaded bracelets, anklets and enormous, elaborate necklaces stretching to their shoulders and in a couple of cases almost down to their elbows. In their language – Maa – Samburu means butterfly, a reflection on the ornate way that they like to dress and bejewel themselves. The women's heads were shaved, and they wore either plastic sandals or flip flops. In those arid conditions with the intense heat, the sparseness of vegetation and water, their lives must be geared totally towards their survival and that of their families. The thought crossed my mind of how little time they must need to worry about appearance. No long hours in front of the mirror with creams and lotions, no wrestling with rollers or heated tongs. No worrying about which style to wear. No cramping feet into pointy-toed shoes or high heels. The other thought that sprang to mind was: How do they keep their clothes so clean and bright? That instantly reminded me of the old Omo advertising jingle: 'Omo washes not only clean, not only white, but bright, Omo adds bright bright brightness'. If they were having to wash their clothes in the river, how did they manage? All the women looked fit and healthy, not muscular like the men, but with no surplus fat so it didn't seem as if they had to worry about dieting, either. I felt drab, like a sparrow among a flock of peacocks. And fat.

These tribespeople's lack of fat is due to their high-protein diet, which is mainly a mixture of blood and milk. They collect blood by cutting a small nick in a vein in the neck of a cow or camel, then plug the wound with ash. Although it's something I wouldn't like to see, I have been told, and believe, that it is not particularly distressing to the animal, no more than for a human giving blood. Mixed with milk, this has been a staple of the Samburu and Maasai tribes, together with various roots that they dig out of the ground. Nowadays, with modern transport methods enabling them to reach local markets, they are beginning to include dried legumes and maize meal in their diet. Meat is only eaten on special occasions, and is both a celebration and an enormous sacrifice, as it entails slaughtering one of the cattle that they love so dearly and around whose well-being Samburu life revolves.

Holding hands and singing, the ladies skipped towards us, and as they approached they neatly lassooed us with a necklace around our necks, men and women alike. Even the relatively small necklace I found myself wearing was heavy for its size, and rather scratchy on my pale skin. Still singing, the ladies herded us gently but firmly, as if we are skittish young goats, towards their *manyatta*, where the men took over and Gabriel talked about Samburu culture.

The older men form a council of elders who are the advisers, decision makers and problem solvers in the community, while the role of the younger *moran* is to maintain peace and protect the community from enemies. Their lives have four main stages: birth, circumcision when they are 15, marriage and death.

Where their close relatives the Maasai have begun to adopt more modern ways of life, the Samburu are still holding on to their traditions, one of the most controversial aspects of which is female circumcision. Although the girls are being taught at school that it is dangerous and wrong, nevertheless, said Gabriel, they all wanted to be circumcised because that is their tradition and they were afraid that otherwise they would not find husbands.

(To divert for a moment: In 2007, a group of progressive young Maasai men began playing cricket. As they learned to love the game they formed a team, calling themselves the Maasai Cricket Warriors, and they travel around the world playing cricket matches, dressed not in traditional whites, but in all their tribal finery, using the game to promote their campaign against female genital mutilation and poaching. Their cause is to retain their culture while at the same time abolishing the negative aspects. Like the Isiolo lawn tennis initiative, it sounds unlikely, playing cricket on a dry, dusty patch of land, but the team has flourished. They tour schools spreading the word, and there is now a ladies' team too. Team captain Sonyanga Weblen Ole Ngais says bowling is easy to master, it's just like throwing a spear. Not only are they very brave to risk attracting the wrath of the tribal elders and gods, but there is no question that they are the most outstandingly handsome cricketers you will ever see. There is a link to their Facebook page at the back of this book.)

Gabriel pointed to the gap between his front teeth, and said that almost everyone in their tribe has the same. This is another tradition, done deliberately, so that if somebody is ill, food and medicine can be administered through the gap. Tetanus is prolific wherever there are animal droppings and enters the body through the skin via injuries, even minor abrasions. One of the symptoms is muscle spasms that can cause the facial muscles to lock the jaws, making it impossible to open the mouth, but the gap in the teeth allows nourishment and medication to be administered to the patient. Pulling out the teeth of young boys, and piercing their ears, is also a test to see whether they will be strong and brave enough to bear the pain of circumcision, he continued. Who's glad not to be a young Samburu?

Back to the *manyatta*. As well as looking after the children and domestic animals, cooking and collecting water from the river, Samburu women are responsible for building their houses – squat lozenge-shaped structures about 5 feet in height, made from a framework of sticks covered with mud, dung, sheets of corrugated metal and animal hides, and whatever other material they can find, with tiny doorways. The roofs are covered with corrugated cardboard, plastic, old tarpaulins and bits of netting, all anchored in place with lengths of rope, old belts and bungee cords. The Samburu are a semi-nomadic people, pastoralists who move when they need to find fresh grazing for their cattle, so their houses are designed so they can be dismantled and the materials packed onto the donkeys which they keep to carry burdens. The *manyattas* leave behind no scars on the environment, and in a short time nature will have erased all sign that they were ever there. The women also make the intricately designed beadwork jewellery, which must be a huge strain on their eyesight, the beads being so tiny and each one having to be individually threaded onto the wire that forms the shape of the finished articles.

I asked Gabriel how the men occupy themselves, because from what he had said so far it sounded as if there was not much left in the way of chores after the women had done a day's work. He replied that the men guard the precious herds and the people from predators and thieves, give advice, and build the '*bomas*' – thick fences made from branches of the prickly acacia thorn trees, which surround the *manyatta*. These thick spiky branches must be extremely disagreeable to handle, so I was pleased to know that this is something the ladies were not expected to do.

An elderly man sat in the shade of one of the houses, beside a young goat busily nibbling at the roof and trying to eat a bungee cord. Outside the thorny walls, a couple of women, upright and elegant, wearing red bead necklaces that reached half way down their upper arms were steering a convoy of plump donkeys laden with plastic bottles towards the river about a quarter of a mile away.

The young warriors take great trouble with their appearance, and grow their hair long, smearing it with ochre to form red locks that they protect with heavy-duty hairnets. They adorn themselves with all kinds of ornately patterned beadwork jewellery, metallic objects, golden chains draped over their ears and around their chins, feathers and plastic flowers, anything that will embellish their appearance. It hardly seems necessary as they are blessed by nature and honed by lifestyle with magnificent physiques and handsome features, and in my opinion the most beautiful men of any race. The colours of the beads have various significances, but like their tribal structure these are very complex and not something which we could learn in a couple of hours. They trade sheep to pay for their beads and fabrics, and use motorbikes for travelling to markets, post offices and pharmacies in nearby towns, which aren't very near at all.

Gabriel's colleague, who stood out from the rest by his slightly rotund appearance, took us to inspect the village. He also spoke perfect English, and when we asked how he learned, he laughed and said that as a youngster he was very bad at looking after the herds and so he was sent to school. From the size of his girth, I suspected he did not live there and share the tribal lifestyle, but came for these occasions to act as a guide.

As well as the houses, within the thorn walls were smaller enclosures where the sheep, goats and chickens were kept during the night to keep them safe from nocturnal predators.

We were invited into one of the homes through a hobbit-sized doorway, requiring us to bend almost in half to get through. Inside it was extremely claustrophobic, with the cramped conditions, low roof, and lack of lighting apart from small holes in the walls, some of which are to allow ventilation, and others plugged with old plastic bags. The interior was divided into two sections by an inner partition. There was a single mosquito net, provided, we were told, by a local mission to protect the very small children, and our guide told us that goat droppings are packed into the walls to act as a deterrent to mosquitos. A plank of wood straddled what look like two empty gas cylinders to form a primitive table, on which stood the only other item in the house, an ancient battered kettle.

In one corner some charcoal embers smouldered, and we were all choking from the smoke. The dirt floor was cleanly swept, and four of our party sat on it in the main 'room' the other side of the partition. Even though I was closest to the door and could see daylight, I still had to fight not to panic. I was crouched uncomfortably, my knees audibly protesting, and one of the men brought a polished, empty 5 pound tin can about 8 inches high and put it on the floor beside me, patting it and gesturing that I should sit upon it. I knew exactly what was going to happen, but it would have been discourteous to refuse his gesture, so I squatted down, balanced as much of one buttock as possible on it, and inevitably toppled off and rolled over. Any dignity I might once have had had long since been abandoned when I found I was bra-less and make-up less, so my only concern was falling against the partition, knocking it down and having the whole structure cave in on us. However, it was obviously far more robust than it looked, as it withstood the impact. As a house, it would take some time to adapt to living in, but on the other hand I think how little time you'd have to spend on housework. No windows to clean, no carpets to beat, no tiles to polish, no need for heating. It did have quite a lot going for it.

Back outside, temporarily blinded between the glare of the sun and the glare of the white earth, we moved across to the school room – a patch of earth beneath a tree where 26 young children sat on the ground dressed in a ragged assortment of grubby clothes. They sang for us with a slight air of bewilderment, as if they were anxious not to forget their lines. They looked well fed and healthy, apart from one very young child wearing a thick mustard-yellow woolly hat; its eyes were watery and it had a runny nose. I heard somebody remark: 'Why don't they clean that child's nose?' I could think of three reasons: tissue handkerchiefs would be a luxury item, fabric handkerchiefs would need washing (remember how little water these people have), and my recollection of runny noses is that they keep running until they eventually dry up.

'Did you bring paper and pencils for the children?' asked one of the men.

We were all abashed, because although everybody had indeed brought these items and more for the slum school we would visit later on our trip, nobody had brought anything today. There was an embarrassed silence.

Our plump friend intervened and steered us over to where a group of *moran* were going to demonstrate their traditional dancing, which is accompanied by chanting and hand clapping. There are no musical instruments. Samburu dancing primarily consists of the men jumping as high into the air as possible. They kicked off their shoes and took it in turns to do so, leaping very high, bending their heels up behind them, and seemed to enjoy themselves. Those who weren't dancing stood in their typical cross-legged stance, with long sticks jutting out between their legs in a somewhat suggestive way. I don't know why they do that, but there is obviously a reason because you see it wherever there are Maasai and Samburu. While they were dancing, a vehicle drove up quickly, and braking fast kicked up clouds of choking dust. We all coughed and spluttered, trying to brush it away from our clothes and faces, but the tribespeople seemed to be impervious and kept up their singing and dancing, which we were watching through a dusty beige veil.

Our hosts invited us to dance. You already know about my bra-less state, and I mentioned earlier that I had packed large clothes to cope with my fluctuating weight. However, shortly before we had left for our trip, my medication seemed to have sorted itself out and I was now losing weight. Consequently all my trousers were far too large, and every time I stood up they threatened to slither down over my hips. I didn't have anything to use as a belt, and neither did Terry, so I always needed one free hand to hold them up. The very last thing I planned on doing was dancing with the Samburu warriors with my trousers around my ankles, so I waved my camera indicating that dancing was not on my agenda. And there's one more thing: Samburu ladies don't jump, but dance by shuffling around while throwing their chests up and down so that their necklaces bounce; remember that I did not have a bra.

The warriors took the ladies from our group – Jessica, Peggy, Cindy, Beth, Jill and Deb – all of whom had clothes that fitted – by the hand and led them in a hoppy-skippy way around in a circle a few times, and then posed for photographs.

I had great admiration for Cindy. An operation on her hand had gone badly wrong leaving irreversible damage, and she had to have something the size of a matchbox implanted in her side, which connected wires into her brain to control the permanent pain caused by the failed operation. The implant had reached the end of its life and was due for replacement in a couple of weeks time when she returned home. The rough roads had made travelling uncomfortable for her, but she bore it like a real trooper, always cheerful and never complaining. She drew a short straw for the dance, because among all the extraordinarily handsome young warriors it was her bad luck to be chosen by an older one who was not even slightly handsome and looked as if there was a bad smell under his nose.

Samburu dancers

After that we moved on to the serious part of our visit – the shopping. Gabriel explained that everything was made on a co-operative basis and sold for the benefit of the whole community. The first 'shop' was a semi-circle of small metal objects displayed on the earth beneath a tree, where the blacksmith crouched. There was nothing there to tempt us, and I felt excruciatingly embarrassed as we all traipsed past barely glancing at the results of this man's handiwork.

The main 'shop' was a collection of ladies sitting on the ground in a horseshoe shape – about 30 of them. In front of them, also on the ground, was the beaded jewellery they had made. Heaps of it. How many beads could there be, all laboriously threaded to form intricate designs? How many hours of work had gone into those creations? Each lady held out her hands, begging us to buy her wares. Incongruously, a mobile phone rang from one of the little hobbit houses, and one of the women scrambled to her feet and ran to answer it.

They all called out to us, trying to make eye contact, imploring us to buy, waving their goods in our faces. I already had the shell necklace I'd bought from the silver-tongued devil, as well as the two necklaces and six bracelets from Isiolo, but the pressure was tangible and it was tacitly understood that everybody would buy something after the hospitality we had been shown, although we had paid for our tour.

Nobody was getting out of here empty-handed. One of the *moran* came over to us and launched his sales pitch, and we were no match for him. The necklace around my neck wasn't going anywhere, except with me. We 'discussed' the price for the necklace, and offered what we were prepared to pay, which was less than he suggested but what Vivien said was a fair price. He shook his head and said that it was far too low, and we said it was all we could afford, so off he went and spoke to an elder. They both looked at us and then turned away and spoke again. After a couple of minutes he came back and said that reluctantly they were prepared to accept our offer, but they felt it was a very mean price and nobody would make any money out of it. On the other hand, he rejected my offer to return it. We tried to convince him that it truthfully was all we could afford to spend, but as Terry took out his wallet I saw the man's eyes on the stack of notes inside. To him it probably looked like a fortune, but he didn't realise that everywhere we went we would be tipping porters and waiters and quite probably having to buy more beaded necklaces. Our funds were already stretched and had to last for the rest of our stay.

I wondered what they thought of us, a group of Westerners who must have seemed, to them, to be wealthy beyond their imagination. I have to be truthful and say that I found this whole episode extremely uncomfortable, as if we had insulted those people, and I wished we could simply have spent time with them as they went about their daily lives, rather than watching them putting on tourist theatre and having to wheedle money from us.

Gabriel and his plump companion remained smiling and courteous, and led us over to watch two *moran* making fire. They had a pointed finger-thick stick, a flat piece of wood with a hole in it, and a small pile of dried dung. One of the men held the hole-stick in place over the dung, while the other man inserted the pointed end of the finger-stick into the hole. Then he rotated it quickly between the palms of his hands for two or three minutes, until a small wisp of smoke curled from the dung. Crouching down, he blew gently onto the wisp, and as the dung began to smoulder he laid over it a handful of dried grass and *voila*! Fire.

I came away from this visit feeling rather uncomfortable and guilty, as if we had been a disappointment to the people, that we had not been sufficiently generous. I'd enjoyed seeing them in their traditional environment and clothing in a world where the business suit and jeans have become the uniform of the masses, and local architectures have succumbed to glass and concrete skyscrapers, but I couldn't see how and for how long they would be able to maintain their lifestyle in a world that is changing so fast.

Robinson Lopunya Kilemuna is a young Samburu student at the Kenya Wildlife Service Training Institute, the only paramilitary institution that trains students in wildlife conservation, tourism, environmental management and fisheries in Kenya. He is taking a course in Natural Interpretation and Tour Administration. His college expenses are paid by Vivien, who shares and supports his passion to save wildlife from extinction, especially in the northern part of Kenya alongside Samburu National Reserve.

It is, he says, really a hard life for the Samburu, but just as 'Elephants always know how to carry their tusks, despite the fact that they are heavy,' his people also know how to survive their hardships. He realises that his community is reliant on tourism in order to improve their lives, and his ambition is to encourage them to change from keeping herds of livestock that stress and interfere with wildlife, and to focus on becoming wildlife conservationists. Tourists not only bring cash, they also come to help in terms of medical aid and practical assistance.

There is something particularly beguiling about that region. At first the barren landscape appears hostile and inhospitable with its absence of greenery. There is little colour, everything is beige and hard, prickly and dry. However, the wildlife is varied and abundant. We had seen some of Kenya's rarest and most elusive animals. The air is so pure, the light is so clear, the people are so beautiful. The contrast between their way of life and ours is a reminder of how lucky we are in terms of comfort and security, but when it comes to freedom and community spirit, and closeness and understanding of how to live with nature, they are light years ahead of us.

That evening we watched elephants scraping disconsolately at the dry sand on the river bed, and I wondered how long it would be before the rains came bringing the water that is vital for the wildlife that can only survive for just so long on night-time dew and moisture from leaves.

Chapter Eighteen

SPEAK SWAHILI: LEO – TODAY

After three days in the parched north-east, we headed west to Nakuru. It was the eighth day of our trip, and it felt as if our stay would last forever. We had been able to tick off in our little green book all of the Samburu Special Five: the Beisa Oryx, the long-necked Gerenuk, the Reticulated Giraffe, the Somali Ostrich and Grévy's Zebra.

As we drove away from the lodge at 5.30am, we were treated to a magical scene – a family of elephants with young, outlined in the golden light of sunrise as they trod purposefully and silently through the scrub.

An armed police escort fell in at either end of our convoy as we neared the outskirts of Isiolo, to ensure our smooth passage through the area where the tribal disturbances had taken place when we arrived, but we saw no sign of any trouble.

When we arrived in town, there was a welcoming committee waiting for Vivien: traders who wanted her to take their goods back to the United States to sell them. They thrust at her metal bracelets and necklaces of red amber beads the size of plums, which she handed to me and I put into a plastic bag. There was no paperwork involved, it was all done on trust. While she was surrounded by still more people waving tons of beaded and amber jewellery, the Somali lady who had invited Michael for a drink hadn't forgotten him.

'Michael – come and have a drink with me now,' she said, pushing her face into the window.

'No, not today,' he smiled.

115

'Michael, my dear, you promised! Have you forgotten your promise to me? You said when you came back. Now you have come back. You promised me.'

Michael laughed, and said, 'No, I didn't promise you anything. Maybe another time.'

'When are you coming back? Are you coming back very soon? Give me your cell phone number so I can call you.'

Michael kept smiling and shaking his head, but she was tenacious and still calling after us as we drove away.

Our route westward took us to Nanyuki, where we stopped slap bang wallop on the Equator. We had, of course, already straddled it during our stay at the Mount Kenya Safari Club, but this was the 'official' place for tourists to have their photo taken beneath a large board to show everybody that they had indeed stood upon the equator.

We managed to avoid being coerced or sweet-talked into the curio shops, because I really couldn't handle any more necklaces for the time being.

A man was demonstrating the Coriolis effect – water going down the plug hole in opposite directions depending upon which hemisphere it is in. His equipment was a plastic bowl with a hole in the centre, which represented a sink and plughole. Beneath the bowl was a bucket to collect the water – a precious commodity and not to be wasted. When he had our attention he poured water from a bottle into the bowl, and placed a matchstick in the water. As the water began to drain away the matchstick twirled lazily in a clockwise direction on the southern hemisphere side of the equator, and on the northern side it whirled anti-clockwise. Right on the line of the equator the matchstick floated motionless. The further away he went from the equator, the faster the matchstick twirled. I'd heard many times that this is a trick, obtained by tilting the bucket or the basin slightly to get the desired effect. I don't know if that is true or not; I'm not a scientist. However, it worked when we watched and was worth giving the man Kenyan Shillings 100 ($1, or GBP 0.60) for his time.

Thomson's Falls is a popular place for tourists coming to visit the waterfall – almost 250 feet of water gushing onto the rocky floor of the valley below, which was named after the 19th century Scottish explorer Joseph Thomson, who also gave his name to the pretty Thomson's gazelle. In his lengthily-titled book *Through Masai Land: a Journey of Exploration Among the Snowclad Volcanic Mountains and Strange Tribes of Eastern Equatorial Africa*, Thomson describes how he convinced the Maasai that he was a powerful medicine man.

'I will show you a thing or two. You see my teeth. Observe how firm they are.' (Here I tapped them with my knuckles). 'You see there is no fraud there. Just wait then till I turn my head. Now look! They are gone!' Here every one shrunk back in intense amazement, and the whole party were on the point of flight. Reassuring them, I once more turned my head, put matters to rights in a twinkling, and, bowing and smiling to my wondering spectators, I once more rapped the teeth. Here let me inform the gentle reader (in the strictest confidence, of course) that I have a couple of artificial teeth, which at this juncture were perfect treasures. These I manipulated to the astonishment of the Masai, and as they thought I could do the same thing with my nose or eyes, they hailed me at once as a veritable white medicine-man.'

This strategy had certain repercussions for Thomson, as at the time the Maasai cattle were dying in great numbers, and his hosts demanded that he use his magical powers to save them before they would let him leave. He wrote of the terrible distress of the people and he feared for his life if he was unable to save them. He resolved his predicament by repeating the tooth trick at hourly intervals, and convincing them that his magic cure would only take effect after ten days, and when he was no longer in their neighbourhood.

Back in the 1960s, the parents of one of my friends farmed at Thomson's Falls. They were gentle, kind people who had built their house with their own hands. It was wood panelled and parquet floored, elegant, with ancestral paintings on the walls and great log fires at night. They cared for their labour force and there was no strife. They provided medical care, housing and education for their workers and their families, and they loved their land and the country of Kenya.

Under the post-Independence Land Settlement Act their farm was compulsorily purchased and divided into small farms for African farmers. I think it broke their hearts, because they moved to England and were both dead within three years.

My friend and I went back two years later to visit the farm. It was a sad sight. The windows were papered over; charcoal fires burned on the parquet; the wood panelling had been removed and used for firewood. Goats and chickens wandered through the desolate rooms. Outside, where coffee had grown in orderly rows, there were patches of maize and bananas, but most of the land had returned to uncultivated bush. A few people waved to my friend and called out to her, but mostly they sat around with a despondent air, as if wondering what they were meant to do with their windfall. What they needed was the knowledge of how to make best use of the land; without it, they were lost.

Thomson's Falls is now known as the slightly-difficult-to-pronounce Nyahururu. What we saw of the town centre was neat and orderly, remnants of its colonial past evident in many of the buildings. It's the highest town in Kenya at over 7,500 feet – a favourite place for Kenyan marathon runners to train as well as being a centre for a thriving floricultural and horticultural industry. The area seemed prosperous, the people well-dressed, smiling, noisy. It looked very different from the slightly dozy little place I remembered.

Dedan owns a dairy farm there, and he had arranged to stop off briefly to meet his family outside Barclays Bank.

By this time we had begun to know our guides well, particularly Dedan as he was the guide we travelled with most frequently. He was the more serious of our four guides, his humour drier, his smile understated. He had a rather majestic and laid back demeanour, and if I was asked to describe him in a single word, it would be 'cool'. On that morning, we saw another side to him, as he hugged his elegant wife Rose, their cute, shy little boy of seven, and their daughter, a stunning teenager carrying the family's latest member, a baby boy. Dedan introduced them all, and they obligingly posed for family photos. In two days' time, Rose's father would be buried. I offered her my condolences, and she was quite pragmatic.

'My father had diabetes for 20 years,' she said. 'It was his time to go.'

I said that it must be an especially difficult time for her, having to attend the funeral without her husband. 'It is all right,' she replied. 'We will manage. Dedan has his work to do.'

As we drove away from Nyahururu, I asked: 'Dedan, were you named after Dedan Kimathi?'

He looked me at sideways, with an inscrutable smile.

During the Mau Mau uprising of the 1950s, one of the most feared and charismatic leaders of the freedom fighters was Dedan Kimathi, known as Field Marshall Kimathi, a handsome man wearing leopard skins and dreadlocks. He was captured in 1956, and hanged in 1957 not as a terrorist, but for being in illegal possession of a firearm, which at the time was a capital offence. He was 37 years old, and on his death he became a hero and martyr.

Six years later, Kenya became independent and Hardinge Street, a major city centre road in Nairobi, was renamed Kimathi Street in his memory. Who Hardinge was, I have no idea, but everybody who lived in Kenya during that era knows the name Dedan Kimathi.

We turned southwards towards our next location, Lake Nakuru Lodge. I ask Dedan what awaited us there. 'Aesthetic value,' he replied enigmatically.

Chapter Nineteen

SPEAK SWAHILI: KESHO – TOMORROW

After a stretch of bumpy track, we arrived at the lodge built in traditional Kenyan style of timber and stone with *makuti* roofs. The porters led us down brick paths, through luscious formal gardens to our rooms, which were quite far from reception. We passed a sparkling swimming pool, and followed zig-zag pathways bordered with towering candelabra euphorbias, varieties of palm trees, colourful shrubs and flowerbeds. There were birds everywhere, flying from tree to tree, singing, and foraging beneath the shrubs and on the lawns. It was absolutely beautiful.

Our rooms were bright, clean and comfortable, with spectacular views out onto the plains. We were used to splendid buffet-style meals, and Lake Nakuru Lodge didn't disappoint.

I mentioned earlier that fancy decoration, gilded mirrors and stuffy furniture are not to my taste. All the places we stayed at had three things in common: gorgeous ethnic architecture and decoration coupled with supreme comfort, five-star food and service that was always attentive and delivered with a smile.

Another thing that pleased me was that our guides all ate in the dining room as guests and were able to enjoy the same food that we did, although later on I learned that this possibly this was not quite the treat I imagined.

Until relatively recently, all safari guides were '*mzungus*' – white people, and Africans only went on safaris as porters or spotters. Spotters travelled on the safari vehicles from a vantage point where their job was to find animals for the guide. When they saw something they would signal it in code, so that it appeared that it was the guide who had seen it. The spotter would not say '500 yards to your right there's a lion.' Instead they would speak in Swahili so that guests could not understand the conversation. All animals had Swahili codes. '*Kulia kwako iko kichwa*' – 'There's a head on your right', 'head' being the code word for a lion, due to the way its head looks large because of its mane. The rhino was *pembe* – horn; elephant was *masikio* – ears, cheetah *madoadoa ya chini* – spotted one on the ground, leopard – *madoadoa ya juu* – spotted one up there.

That has changed, with many spotters having worked their way up to become highly qualified guides, taking clients not only all over Kenya but also to the neighbouring countries of Tanzania, Uganda, Rwanda, and even Ethiopia, and in a neat little twist, *mzungus* now promote native Kenyan tour companies.

From the dining room, we looked out onto a waterhole 50 yards away where a zebra was either drinking or admiring its reflection. Close by, a muddy buffalo sunbathed in the grass, and on a table beside us an iridescent Ruppell's glossy starling, dressed in metallic blue and purple feathers was clearing up the crumbs.

The landscape here is lush and verdant, in contrast to the glaring whiteness of Amboseli and the golden scrub of Samburu. Lake Nakuru is a haven for wild birds and paradise for bird watchers. On our afternoon drive, we were rewarded with the sight of a trio of Southern ground hornbills strutting around purposefully, close to the vehicle, jabbing and prodding into the long grass in search of snacks – insects, amphibians, reptiles, carrion and even small mammals. At 3 feet tall, they are the largest hornbills in the world, with sleek black plumage and a very large lethal beak. Their dramatic crimson wattles and 'spectacles' around their eyes make them ideal for posters advertising horror films.

The sunlight caught on the luminous powdery green of the bark on a grove of acacia xanthophloea, commonly known as the yellow fever tree. Early white settlers who camped beneath these attractive trees would frequently develop malaria or yellow fever. These acacias favour wet marshy areas, which coincidentally is the preferred habitat of mosquitos which, also coincidentally, are vectors for malaria and yellow fever. Although this message was eventually received and understood, and the tree was absolved of any responsibility, the accusatory name lingers on. I detected a mild snort of scorn from Dedan.

We had debated long and hard whether or not to take anti-malarial medication on our trip, and been given conflicting advice. Our French doctor – who has a horror of flying, insects, wild animals and exposure to sun – was aghast that (a) we'd even consider visiting Africa and (b) we'd travel on an aeroplane. In his opinion, we would be virtually committing suicide, and certainly we would succumb to malaria amongst a host of other potentially fatal diseases if we didn't crash or get eaten by lions first.

People said the risks of catching the disease were too high to take any chances. Other people said the medication could have horrible side-effects and wasn't 100% reliable. Vivien had assured us that everywhere we stayed we would be well-protected in our rooms by netting, and that provided we covered up after sundown we were most unlikely to be bitten. After much thought, we opted not to take any prophylaxis to add to the already essential medications we took. In the evenings, we wore long-sleeved tops, long trousers and socks, and applied a mild deterrent cream to our faces and necks (Avon Skin So Soft Body Spray). The whole time we were there, I only saw one mosquito. Which I promptly despatched, because much as I dislike killing anything, I didn't want us to risk malaria, nor be kept awake by the intensely irritating whine that these little creatures make. Neither of us suffered any insect bites.

A herd of Cape buffalo emerged from the yellow fever copse, and stood in the afternoon sunshine looking slightly dozy, as if they hadn't fully woken up from an after-lunch nap yet. They stand 5 feet at the shoulder and weigh up to 1,500 pounds. With their curved horns they looked huge until a couple of white rhino appeared and started grazing near them. Seeing these gigantic, prehistoric-looking creatures close to the buffalo put their size into perspective – they made the buffalo look like toys. We were close enough to the animals to count the flies around their eyes and nostrils. Despite their reputations as unpredictable, aggressive and vindictive, both groups ignored us, intent only on helping themselves to the rich green grasses. After decades of mass tourism, protected in the parks and reserves and knowing they have nothing to fear from mankind (except, of course, the poachers) most of the animals are generally quite relaxed and undisturbed by the close presence of human beings and vehicles.

Did you know that the collective noun for warthogs is a sounder, and that their babies are called hoglets, and that they have to kneel down to eat because a design flaw by nature made their necks too short, and that one of their preferred places to sleep is in abandoned aardvark burrows? Knowing this, lions just have to sit and wait for them to come out. See how much you can learn in a few minutes?

Dedan pointed to a nondescript shrub bearing yellow berries. It's called Sodom's apple, said to be the first plant to grow after the destruction of the cities of Sodom and Gomorrah. It's a member of the solanum family, a relative of deadly nightshade and a thoroughly nasty plant, bitter in taste, invasive and toxic to humans, sheep and cattle. However native antelope can eat it without ill-effect, and so can elephants, which is useful in as much as there is less for the domestic farm animals, but the seeds are dispersed in droppings, enabling the shrub to spread to the detriment of beneficial grasses. For Kenyan farmers it represents a threat to their livestock, but paradoxically trials are being carried out to test its efficiency as a pesticide and insecticide, destroying aphids on one of Kenya's staple crops – kale, and controlling parasites on cattle. It's a double-edged sword of a plant.

When we returned from our drive, the accumulation of weeks of anticipation and anxiety, the long journey here, and the early mornings had caught up with me. I was feeling fragile. I just wanted to lie on the comfortable bed in the delicious room and rest for a few hours, so I decided to miss dinner and catch up on some sleep. I asked Terry to bring me something to eat when he came back, flopped onto the bed and was instantly asleep. Some time later, I was awakened by a persistent tapping at the door. Thinking that Terry had forgotten his key, I opened it to find a smiling nurse standing there.

'Joseph Muya heard that you were not feeling well. He has sent me to make sure you are OK.'

Joseph is the owner of Lake Nakuru Lodge, and an old friend of Vivien's since the days when she was breeding racehorses and he was working as a groom. From a poor childhood, he had taken every opportunity that came his way, and worked himself up to become a jockey, racehorse breeder and trainer, hotelier, businessman and a director of the Jockey Club of Kenya. He says that his success is due to his love of horses, as they inspired him with their determination to win.

Gently ignoring my protests that all I needed was a good long sleep, the nurse took my temperature and blood pressure and squeezed my ankles. We agreed that there was nothing much wrong but she would come back to check again the following day. Terry returned with a plate of cheese and biscuits and some fruit. After I'd eaten, I laid back down, but sleep didn't come because ever since that stop in Nyahururu there had been a small niggling thought in the back of my mind, and now it had jumped to the front.

When we came to live in Kenya in 1954, I was a young child. As a family we instantly fell in love with the country. It seemed entirely natural to us that white people lived in beautiful houses and drove cars, while Kenyans worked for us and either walked, rode on bicycles or travelled by lethal buses or taxis. I am quite sure that at least for the first few years this way of life seemed perfectly normal and we did not question the justice of it. Living in Kenya was paradise for us. We had left behind a grey house in a grey street in a London suburb, and thirteen years of rationing of clothes, petrol, soap, butter, meat, sugar, sweets, in fact pretty much everything that wasn't essential. My mother had somehow managed to feed us nutritiously and clothe us during that time. Now she could relax. We lacked for nothing, and our new lifestyle seemed the height of luxury. The motorbike and sidecar that had been my father's pride and joy in England – where we had been the only people in our street who owned a motorised vehicle – was replaced with a stately Vauxhall Velox with leather upholstery. The weather was perfect. The food was plentiful. We had space, leisure time, money and servants.

But not all was well in Kenya at that time, because in 1952 the Governor had declared a State of Emergency in response to the Mau Mau uprising. As a child I had no idea what it was about, although I was aware that there was something which concerned us as white people. I do recall that the attitude amongst our community was one of fear of what might happen to us, and extreme indignation that our position should be threatened.

Adults spoke quietly amongst themselves, discussing the possibility that the cook or gardener may be a 'Mickey Mouse' – a euphemism for Mau Mau. The Emergency was that the people to whom this country rightfully belonged now wanted to run it themselves. To Europeans, it was all very alarming. We might be killed in our beds. Every black face could belong to a freedom fighter, or terrorist as they were known.

It was a horrible period for Kenya. The main tribe behind the Mau Mau was the Kikuyu, and you were either with them – a Mau Mau supporter and fighter – or against them, which made you the enemy. While a number of Europeans were killed during the Emergency, many more loyal Kikuyu – those who did not support the Mau Mau – were killed.

I lay thinking about British history in Kenya. The country had evolved from a Protectorate to a colony in a few decades. A Protectorate is defined as a powerful state undertaking to protect a weaker one. I'm not a historian, I don't understand how that worked, who gave their agreement to this arrangement, whether the population at large had any say in it, and who or what they were being protected from.

In 1920, Kenya's status was changed from Protectorate to Colony governed by British law. Again, I wondered how this was negotiated. It opened up the country to settlers who began to arrive and establish themselves in prime agricultural areas. Nyahururu, or Thomson's Falls as it was called then, is part of what was known as the White Highlands, millions of acres of the most fertile land in the country. Many of the British settlers were from the aristocracy, or British army officers, people sufficiently wealthy to purchase and develop vast areas of such land. The native Kenyan inhabitants were displaced and confined to smaller and less productive areas, with the most profitable land reserved exclusively for whites.

Kenyans were moved into reserves and obliged to carry identity cards – *kipandes* – to keep track of their movements. They were discouraged from growing those crops that were most profitable – coffee, tea and sisal. In three decades, the

African way of life was subordinated to British culture, British laws, British clothing, British buildings. They even had a new god and a new official language.

The settlers needed labour to work on their farms, on their roads, in their factories and in their homes. To 'encourage' the native Kenyans to work for them, the government imposed a tax on their homes – the hut tax which could be paid either in money, or in labour. Either way, the only way to pay it was to work for the settlers.

The settlers were only taking advantage of the opportunity offered to them; they weren't responsible for the actions of their government. They passionately loved the country and put their hearts and souls into it. Many left when Independence arrived, but there are still families living there whose ancestors arrived over a hundred years ago and created farms, industries and resorts to create the modern prosperous country that Kenya is today. They regard it as home, and themselves as Kenyans every bit as much as the indigenous population.

I kept going back to the question of how we – the British – gained the right to 'own' this land. If we asked Kenyans today whether they felt that our presence had been beneficial to them, or given the choice would they have kept to their own way of life and culture, what would they say? Western technology, education and medicine have brought many benefits, but are also at least partly responsible for one of the greatest problems facing Kenyans today – over-population.

It's easy to understand why we wanted to live here in this beautiful country and I thought things may have turned out otherwise if we had come and settled peacefully instead of making the people to whom the country belonged second class and third-rate citizens. Africans were not admitted to certain clubs and restaurants except as staff, and up until the 1960s it was unusual for whites to socialise with black Kenyans. There was an arrogance and lack of empathy among some of the whites who referred to old men as 'boys', and worse, and there was a deep lack of understanding.

For some reason I remembered Edward, our office messenger, a quiet, fairly elderly man judging by his greying hair. In the time he worked for the company, I only heard him ever speak one word, and that was '*Ndio*' – yes. I always spoke to him in English, which he understood perfectly, and he always replied in Swahili.

His duties included trips to the post office to collect and deliver post, shopping errands for office supplies and snacks, and collecting cash from the bank on the floor below the office. He also made tea, and despite me showing him many times how it should be made, he had his own method which he adhered to. That was to put the tea leaves, milk and sugar into the electric kettle and let it boil furiously for several minutes and nothing I said could change it. That is the way Kenyans like their tea.

'You put the tea leaves in this pot,' I said for the twentieth time. 'Then boil just the water in the kettle and pour the boiling water into the pot. Leave it in the pot for a few minutes, and then pour it into cups and add the milk and sugar.' '*Ndio*,' he replied. He knew how he wanted his tea made, and that's how he did it. I found the result quite unpleasant, especially as I didn't take sugar, and it did the kettle no good at all.

My boss was tolerant of Edward's tea-making foibles. He was also generous – when we had cakes or snacks, Edward was included. But there was a problem. Edward always arrived wearing a thick green military greatcoat, even during the hottest season. He hung it neatly in the lobby. The problem was that it smelt very strongly of perspiration, and so did Edward. My boss gave me the excruciatingly embarrassing task of talking to Edward about personal hygiene. I bought him a packet of bars of soap, which he took politely and I said as diplomatically as I could that he should use it each day before he came to work. '*Ndio*,' he said.

The problem did not go away, however, and it came to the point where my boss was saying that Edward would have to go, because the odour was offending visitors. It was clear that Edward was not making use of the soap.

One morning, the boss called me into his office.

'Did you know,' he asked, 'that Edward walks to work every day, from Langata?'

That was a distance of nearly 10 miles. He continued: 'I passed him on the road early this morning, so I gave him a lift. He told me,' (apparently Edward could speak English perfectly well when he chose) 'that he walked to save money on bus fares so he could send it to his family instead. And the reason he wears his greatcoat every day is because it's his most valuable possession, and there is nowhere he can leave it where he lives without the risk of it being stolen. When I asked him about the soap he told me that he has no running water, just a small bowl of cold water from a communal stand pipe to wash and shave in.'

He continued: 'Learn a lesson from this. Don't assume anything about anybody. We don't know how other people live.'

After that, he increased Edward's wages to cover his bus fares, but I suspect he continued walking those twenty miles a day to earn his wages and save more money for his family, because the problem didn't go away.

Edward solved it himself after he had been with the company for just under a year, when one day he failed to return from the bank with the petty cash – quite a sizeable sum by his standards. And that was the last we saw of him, as he had high-tailed it back to his home far from Nairobi. When I explained that the petty cash tin was empty and we no longer had an office messenger, I expected anger or at least indignation from my volatile boss, but he simply shrugged his shoulders and remarked: 'Poor bastard, what can you expect? Too much temptation for a poor man. Who can blame him? The amount isn't going to affect our lives, but I hope it will make a difference to his.'

However, I paid the price for Edward's peccadillo, as I was ultimately responsible for the petty cash and therefore had to replace it myself. However, I received a very large bonus at Christmas. My boss was so unpredictable. :)

I thought what it must have been like, how humiliating and unjust to see Europeans with smart clothes and cars, eating in restaurants, owning large houses with running water and electricity, and yet to be living in poverty in your own country.

It was no surprise that after 70 years, progressive Kenyans had had enough and wanted control of their own country. The two most instantly recognisable names connected with the Mau Mau were Jomo Kenyatta who was accused of masterminding it, and General Dedan Kimathi whose name had set off the chain of thoughts that was keeping me awake.

I clearly remembered the night of 12th December 1963, when Britain handed Kenya back to its people and it became a republic under the presidency of Jomo Kenyatta. Many Europeans had left already, afraid of repercussions, fearing a bloodbath. A friend invited me to stay on their farm far away from Nairobi 'just to be on the safe side.'

So what happened that night?

Joyful celebrations and a rousing speech from Kenyatta – the 'Forgive and forget President' calling for *harambee* – everybody working together to build a new nation. We had nothing to fear, and I remember a multi-racial society where we all lived in harmony, as Kenyans began to take over the running of their country. They showed a remarkable lack of rancour towards we Europeans, something that has always impressed me. Focus was on moving forward, not looking backwards.

There are so many things I don't understand. I don't understand how man can measure the distance to the sun and planets; I don't understand how electricity is made and stored; I don't understand how satellites or gravity work. Not understanding those and many other things doesn't concern me or keep me awake at night. But two things do. One is how any human being can gain pleasure from injuring or killing a living creature. Although I don't eat meat, I appreciate that people kill animals for food, I can understand killing them in self-defence, and as much as I abhor it I can even understand why people kill them to profit from the sale of their coats, horns and tusks. But to kill something that is beautiful just to pose with its body for a photograph, or to mount its head on a wall, or use its skin as a rug, that completely defeats my understanding. It is not even as if there is any skill needed, just sufficient money and an adequate gun. It seems such an utterly pointless and negative activity. As well as local organisations, there are many international institutions working to protect Kenya's dwindling wildlife. This seems to me quite ironic as it was Europeans and Americans who first introduced killing for fun, with their high-powered weapons, from the early explorers who killed or captured whatever they could to take back to museums, zoos or private collections, to the so-called 'great white hunters' behind whose glamorous image were men who made their living and reputation from killing the big game, to those who spend their weekends out shooting and the individuals who facilitate and enjoy canned hunting – killing wildlife that is fenced in to prevent it escaping, and offering a guarantee that the 'hunter' can kill it. When animals were hunted with spears and arrows for food, protection or cultural purposes there was relatively little threat to their long-term survival.

The second thing that keeps me awake is trying to understand how people can hate others purely based on their religion or skin colour. There is no logic in it. There are good people and bad people in every race and of every persuasion.

My mind went into overdrive when I began thinking about how we had created partition in India, and all the endless troubles caused by chopping up the Middle East, and my thoughts whirled around and around in endless circles. Then they hopped to Australia and New Zealand and their dispossessed native populations, and then back to the Pilgrim Fathers and the plight of the American Indians. It seemed to me that wherever we had gone we had abused the original inhabitants, damaged or destroyed their culture, treated them with cruelty and disdain and left behind swathes of chaos and poverty. I visualised the map of the world as it was when I was a small child, with the pink parts that comprised the British Empire covering a quarter of the globe, of which we were taught to be so proud and there I was lying in a bed at Lake Nakuru Lodge pondering how it was that I had never considered the morality of any of it until today.

I did eventually fall asleep and woke next morning with the larks, firing on all cylinders and finally feeling 100%, apart from a disillusionment with our Imperialist history that would very probably never have occurred to me if Dedan had any other name.

We ate breakfast to the accompaniment of a chorus of birdsong, watching through the pearly morning mist as a troop of baboons appeared from a nearby copse of trees. Looking around furtively, they scampered towards the mesh fence designed to keep them out of the grounds of the lodge. It was about as effective as the Maginot line, so the troupe leader made for a particular spot, then with a quick glance around him lifted the fence and crawled beneath it. Others followed him, guilt written all over their monkey faces as they peered about to see if anybody would stop them. In a few moments, they were all safely inside the fence that was meant to keep them out.

Wise, unflappable Kamara was our driver, and we were

sharing the vehicle with animal lovers Mike and Stacey. First stop was Baboon Point, a vantage place on top of a cliff overlooking Lake Nakuru. In the early morning, the still waters lay like a metallic silvery-grey mirror against a backdrop of hazy blue and lilac hills fading out to the horizon. The colours were so soft and muted that the camera could not do them justice, and I wished I could paint to capture their delicate beauty in fifty shades of pinks, greys, blues, silvers and lavenders. While I generally think of Kenya in terms of bold, vivid colours, there are also scenes of ethereal beauty, and this was one of them.

The lake is fed from underground sources and streams from the vast forest covering the Mau escarpment. Two years before our visit, the water level had risen high enough to flood the offices of the the Kenya Wildlife Services, damaging it beyond repair, as well as engulfing roads and parts of the forest. Drowned skeletal trees now stood stark and forlorn in the water, a sad but rather dramatic image. This lake can dry up completely into a dust bowl or change its level to cover anything from two to twenty square miles. Back in the 1960s, I used to come to see the flamingos which lived here in their thousands, feeding on the algae, but frequent flooding diluted the salinity of the water so the algae has diminished and there is no longer sufficient food to support so many birds, so they have mostly migrated north to other lakes.

However, that doesn't mean that there is no bird life on the lake. There is, in abundance. In the 1960s, to control the mosquitos which thrived in the area, the lake was stocked with fish that would eat the mosquito larvae. This has attracted migratory birds like avocets and spotted redshanks, while fish eagles, pelicans and herons are plentiful, all there to eat the fish that were introduced to eat the mosquitos.

Kamara pointed to a small black and white bird that was singing its heart out in a medley of trills, squawks and scales.

'Sooty chats. Very beautiful songs,' he said. Nearby, that avian palette of vibrant colour, the lilac-breasted roller landed on a branch and sat perfectly still until I pointed my camera at it. Then if flew down to the ground, posed again looking straight into my eyes until I had it in focus, and then it was off again in a technicolour blur. I could almost hear it laughing, and never did succeed in capturing a decent photo of this most spectacular little bird.

We stopped beside a leleshwa tree with its cloud of grey, velvety leaves. Kamara picked some and gave each of us a few which we crushed in our hands, releasing a powerful, pleasant antiseptic smell of camphor. The Maasai, he told us, tuck the leaves into their armpits to act as a natural deodorant, and use them as air fresheners in their homes as well as for medicinal purposes.

Kamara is slow moving, gentle, shy and modest. Even when he is smiling, his face shows the hint of a frown, as if he is permanently trying to foresee where the next problem may come from, and how he will deal with it. He is Vivien's right hand man, and he is extraordinarily patient, which he needs to be, because whenever there is something to sort out or advice needed, Vivien will be yelling: 'KAMAAAARA! KAMAAAAAARA!' He will leave whatever he is doing and amble over, bend his head to listen, and amble away to do whatever needs doing. You feel that if you were ever in a sticky situation, as long as Kamara was with you, you'd come out of it OK. He is a married man with four children, loves animals and is an excellent mechanic. If I had to choose one word to describe Kamara, it would be 'wise'.

During lunch, a large man came over to our table and introduced himself. Joseph Muya is the owner of Lake Nakuru Lodge, a jovial man with a soft voice.

'Are you well?' he asked. 'I have been worried about you.'

I thanked him for his concern and for sending the nurse,

assured him that I'd never felt better and was thoroughly enjoying our visit to Lake Nakuru.

'That is very good news,' he said. 'We love to welcome guests to our beautiful park. If you need anything, just ask for me personally and I will make sure that you are kept very happy.'

I think I may have said it before, but Kenyans really do know how to treat their guests and make them feel special, and not simply as customers.

Lake Nakuru is one of the few places where the endangered Rothschild's giraffe can be seen in the wild. Back in our room after lunch, I was sitting by the window looking out onto the plains, when one of these beautiful animals glided past, stopping briefly to scratch its neck on an acacia tree stump. Unlike the fuzzy lines of the Maasai giraffe we saw in the Amboseli park, and the neater patterned reticulated giraffe in the Samburu reserve, the Rothchild's version is somewhat paler, and its pattern only extends down as far as its knees. From there on down its legs are plain and creamy-coloured as if it's wearing long socks, making it quite distinct from its cousins. Each time I saw a giraffe, I felt a pang of sadness and disbelief, remembering the great herds I knew, and reminded that a harmless, beautiful and once prolific animal is on the road to extinction.

Later that afternoon, we drove down to the lake shore where white storks and solemn, undertaker-like marabou prowled through the grass, prodding with their great beaks in search of hapless small creatures. As we already knew, there were very few flamingos to be seen, maybe a hundred at most, but they still formed an elegant sight with their vivid pink plumage reflecting from the surface of the water. They are irrevocably linked in my mind to the croquet mallets in *Alice in Wonderland*.

We wandered around the shore for half an hour, watching the birds and photographing them. It was only as we were making our way back to the vehicles that we noticed that 50 short yards away from where we had been standing, there were four white rhinos – 16,000 pounds of armour-plated animal – snoozing peacefully beneath a clump of trees.

What we had all been hoping for was sight of the elusive black rhino, as this is one of the few locations where it can be found, but we scoured the paths and forests without success. On the other hand, I lost count of the number of birds we saw, and was so busy looking at them I didn't have time to tick them off in the little green book.

That evening we had two treats. The first was a talk from David, a dedicated conservationist, and champion of rhinos, in particular the black rhino, who had given up his evening off to educate and entertain us. He is broad and powerfully built, with a very mobile face that has one of the widest smiles you'll ever see as he tells a joke, but which can quickly change to a look of deep concentration. He had become a guide by accident when he was training as a vet, following in his father's footsteps. While working at a wildlife conservancy, assisting veterinarians from all over the world who came to carry out research and treat wild animals, with his personable manner and driving skills he was asked to take people on guided drives.

He enjoyed doing this so much that he returned to college to study wildlife management and tourism and now holds a coveted silver medal from the Kenya Professional Safari Guides Association. He told us how the previous year he had narrowly failed the exam to become a gold level guide, despite his years of experience and encyclopaedic knowledge. His failure was due to a lack of knowledge concerning East African marine life. He said, somewhat ruefully: 'I haven't had much experience with sharks.'

David has been involved for many years in translocating the endangered black rhino and Rothschild's giraffe to conservancies for their protection. When he's not on safari, he volunteers his time to campaign against poaching, educating the younger generation about their wildlife heritage and the importance of protecting it, and promoting ecological projects such as tree planting. David hopes that one of his daughters will also become a professional safari guide, and is encouraging her in that direction. On top of that, he is a skilled photographer and videographer. One word describes David: 'Passionate'.

We sat outside around a large metal brazier heaped with logs. 'This is what we call African television – the family sitting by the fire in the evenings, talking and telling stories,' David laughed.

I remember that night very clearly, the smell of wood smoke and the faces of our fellow travellers lit by the firelight. We had bonded so well and any worries we had had about not fitting have long been put to rest. All our companions were kind, friendly, enormously enthusiastic and with a great sense of humour, and we could not have chosen a more sociable and likeable group of people to travel with.

David is a good speaker, and knowledgeable on his subject. As he began to talk, I realised how little I actually knew about rhinos.

The first thing I didn't know was that there are six species of rhino, and three of them live in Asia.

The three African species are the black rhino, the southern white rhino and the northern white rhino. White rhino are not white and black rhino are not black. They are both grey. The black rhino is indigenous to Kenya; the white is not.

The 'white' prefix comes from the Afrikaans word for 'wide', a reference to the creatures' blunt, wide mouths which distinguish them from the black rhino which have longish pointy prehensile upper lips similar to a short trunk.

The southern white rhino is native to the southern part of

the African continent, and was once almost extinct. Over the last century they have been translocated to other areas, including Kenya in order to establish new herds. Theirs is a success story, as the population has grown to somewhere in the region of 20,000 in the wild, although they are still vulnerable to poaching and loss of habitat.

Of their cousins the northern white rhino indigenous to the north of the continent, there are only three left in the world. Two of them are sterile females. An animal that can trace its ancestors back more than 50 million years is about to vanish forever, killed off for their horns, to be sold as aphrodisiacs to gullible Asians, and used as scabbards for Yemeni traditional daggers. Imagine. A whole race of animals wiped out by man's greed and stupidity. The three survivors live on a conservancy in Kenya where they are under 24-hour armed guard. The only slender hope of saving them from extinction rests with the scientists who have been harvesting cells from them to try to reproduce them through stem cell technology. If that fails, it will be the end of the northern white rhino.

The white and black rhino although superficially similar are different both physically and behaviourally. White rhino are larger than Kenya's native black rhino, weighing up to 5,000 pounds against 3,000 pounds. They are grazers, favouring the open plains and eating from the ground using their wide, blunt mouths. The smaller and shyer black rhino live in the forests, browsing bushes and twigs with their long lips. While the black rhino always walks ahead of its babies, white rhino parents follow their young. Both species mark their territorial boundaries with their dung, and the two do not socialise.

Their tragic plight worldwide is due to loss of habitat and poaching to feed the Asian market's insatiable and insane lust for rhino horn, which gullible people believe to be an aphrodisiac. The horn is simply a concentrated mass of keratin, the same substance that makes up human hair and fingernails, so they'd achieve the same 'benefit' from eating those. There is no magic ingredient in it. It is the rhino's long-duration mating – up to 90 minutes – that has given foolish people the idea that the horn possesses magical powers, when the real magic is the fortune that cynical traders are making by exploiting their stupidity. Unless they wake up to that fact, there will come a time when there are no longer any rhino horns left, and what are they going to do then? Hey, boys, wake up now – you can get little blue pills from your doctor, cheaper and guaranteed to have the required effect. Stop being taken for fools and wasting your money. Rhino horn costs more than heroin. There is so much money at stake that even those who are paid to protect the animals, and have sworn to do so cannot be trusted. One rhino was found dead, its horn removed, but with no visible injury that could have caused death. An autopsy revealed that it had been tranquilised by a vet, its horn removed and then left to die.

It's all very sobering, the thought that entire species are being destroyed so needlessly, and it is David and people like him, committed to conservation through education, who are the best hope for the rhino's survival.

After dinner, we were invited to listen to a local African choir, the Friends of Lake Nakuru. As we settled down for the performance, the nurse who visited last night arrived with a blood pressure sleeve. 'You were gone when I came to find you this morning,' she said, pumping up my arm and pleased to find that my blood pressure had returned to normal. I asked how I should pay for her services. 'Oh no! You are our guest. We are here to look after you.'

The leader of the choir explained that they would be singing *a capella*, as something has prevented their musicians attending. They had wonderful melodious voices, and sang a selection of old Kenyan favourites – '*Jambo*

Bwana' and '*Malaika*' as well as traditional tribal songs, and when they had finished they started pulling guests up to dance. Bra-less, make-up-less and wearing trousers two sizes too large, they had more chance of getting Nelson's Column to dance than me. I politely declined the gentleman who strode at me with his hand extended, and waved my camera, my first line of defence. When we are out game viewing, I couldn't care less about my appearance – nobody is going to notice it amongst the splendour of the landscape and the wildlife – but I do have my limits.

The lodge's resident watchman escorted us back to our bungalow. He was a rather sad-looking man wearing a couple of glowing red *shukas* and carrying a sturdy *rungu* – the heavy carved wooden club with a large knob that with sufficient force can knock your brains right out of your head – and a lethal-looking catapult hanging around his neck. Now I realise the significance of the catapult seller we saw at Isiolo – they are used as deterrents for unwelcome visitors, as well as for hunting birds and small animals.

This park is a harbour of peace and beauty, and if we were rich, I think we could happily live here forever.

Chapter Twenty

SPEAK SWAHILI: KARIBU – WELCOME

We were on the move again next morning, driving to the Masai Mara where we would be staying in a tented camp for our 'Out of Africa' experience.

It was still dark when we left at 5.30am. The only noise, apart from the low murmurs of the porters taking our bags to the vehicles, was the chirping of the crickets and the song of the birds attracted by the lights. In the black sky, amongst the stars I saw a brilliant red glow that could only be the planet Mars. We were astonished at how clear and red it was, and beckoned all our fellow travellers to come and look. We all clustered around, pointing and inviting more and more people to come and see this extraordinary sight.

One of the porters stopped to ask what we are looking at.

'Mars!' we told him, pointing at the red glow.

He gazed up into the sky. 'That is the light on top of a telecommunications mast,' he said, walking away, his shoulders jiggling and his head shaking as he chuckled to himself at the stupidity of the *mzungu*.

It was another long day drive, and we were riding with Dedan. As well as being an excellent guide, he is also political and up to date with current affairs. Every journey with him was an education. He pointed out a vast tract of land belonging to a European which was lying idle, while local Africans owned no land. A bill had been introduced in the Kenyan parliament to restrict the amount of land an individual could own to 25 acres in areas that are particularly fertile, and in less fertile areas, 60 acres. Any acreage over and above that would be bought by the government for distribution to the landless. While it sounded like a noble idea, I was dubious that even if it ever became law it would lead to an equitable distribution of land, as the wealthiest landowners would find ways to circumnavigate the law – easily done by forming a company – and therefore not count as individuals. I wasn't optimistic.

We were heading south towards Narok. The traffic was a mixture of *boda bodas*, pedestrians, saccos, overloaded dilapidated vehicles with their bumpers scraping the road, *wabenzi* (people driving expensive cars like Mercedes), motorbikes often carrying several passengers or piled up with goods, bicycles and donkey carts. On the roads beside straggles of grazing sheep, goats, baboons and zebra, vendors offered vegetables, eggs, bottled water. Everywhere there were signs pointing to churches and schools. Kenyans are predominantly Christian and passionate about the importance of education to ensure that their children can progress in a modern world.

Dedan pointed to a dismal collection of buildings beside the road. 'IDPs,' he said, as if we should know what an IDP was. As he didn't volunteer, I had to ask.

'IDPs? What is that?'

'Internally Displaced Persons. They are people who have lost their homes for some reason. Sometimes natural disasters, but many of them had to flee for their own safety during the election violence in 2007. These people are living in very bad conditions in these places. They don't have good healthcare, or education, or opportunities to work, and cannot return to their homes.'

As Terry remarked, it was one of those moments when you stop and think how very fortunate we are to have been born where, when and who we are.

We drove past thousands upon thousands of acres of undulating fields of golden wheat and maize. In the movies, Maasai are almost always depicted wearing traditional dress and nudging their cattle across desert wastes. While many of them do still follow a pastoralist lifestyle, others have abandoned tradition and adopted modern ways, turning to agriculture. It was harvest time; already some of the fields had been reduced to stubble, and combine harvesters stood ready for their next assault.

Narok town is a thriving commercial centre, chaotic and lively, the administrative capital of the region and it was particularly busy with the wheat harvest in full swing. Seeing the throngs of people and vehicles, you would not have thought that just a few months earlier the town had suffered one of its frequent destructive floods. Narok sits in a slight depression, so consequently during heavy rains the water rushes down from the surrounding land. Deforestation has worsened the situation, with trees cut down to produce charcoal, and an inadequate drainage system. Four months previously in April, at least 15 people had been swept to their deaths, cars and trucks were washed away, stalls and kiosks destroyed and buildings flooded. This had been followed by even worse floods in May, and would be again in November (after our visit) with further loss of life, property, livestock and ruined infrastructure. Local Government have discussed the possibility of relocating the whole town to higher ground, and although there is resistance from the Maasai who own the land, it's hard to see what other solution is available. A town in a basin just doesn't make sense.

But on that dry sunny day there were no visible signs of the catastrophe. The centre was crowded, hot, noisy and frantically busy, with cars, bikes, buses, pedestrians and donkey carts milling around in every direction. The guides were not keen to stop, but Vivien had decided to stock up on biscuits and sweets for the vehicles. She jumped out of the vehicle and cut through the crowd like Moses parting the Red Sea, while Terry took advantage of the opportunity to buy us all ice cream. Then Vivien decided that the vehicles should be refuelled. As we pulled into the fuel station, we were instantly surrounded by vendors tapping on the windows and waving sunglasses, baseball caps, catapults, belts, T-shirts and sandals. We managed to keep them at bay with smiles and shaking heads, but every exit from the station was blocked with cars and lorries in a complete nose-to-tail gridlock. Some vehicles were trying to get in, others were trying to get out, yet more didn't seem to have any plan but were just parked obstructively. It didn't look as if we'd ever be able to leave, but Dedan edged forward and found a sliver of space for the convoy to wriggle between the other vehicles and onto the road.

I was sitting up in the front, enjoying the ever-changing scenery. We were about a quarter of a mile out of town when an oncoming car swerved suddenly and then there was a small colourful bundle lying in road just ahead of us. At first I thought it was a heap of fabrics, but I was horrified to see a little black arm move feebly from within it. A child had been knocked down. As we came to a halt, a *boda boda* coming from the opposite direction slammed to a stop; the passenger leapt from the bike and snatched up the child, cradling it to his chest and climbing back onto the bike which rushed away towards the nearby hospital.

The little body was limp in the man's arms, the head and limbs dangling. It had all happened so fast, only 20 seconds from the moment we saw the child fall to the bike vanishing. All the vendors and people passing were standing still, staring after the bike. The child's mother who had been selling vegetables beside the road was wailing and tearing at her face.

There was nothing that we could do. The car had stopped and pulled over to the side of the road. It was probably that the child had run across the road and into the side of the car, rather than being hit by it. A driver causing death or injury would usually drive away for fear of being attacked or even

145

killed by bystanders delivering mob justice. The fact that this car had stopped suggested that the driver was not responsible. The police would come to interview the driver and the witnesses, and we could only pray that the child would recover, but we would never know whether or not she did.

As we drove onwards, in my mind I kept seeing that little girl in her colourful clothes, lying there in the road, and the motorbike passenger acting so quickly. I felt tears rolling down my face and leaving a salty taste in my mouth. Inside I was saying: 'Please be all right, little girl, please be all right.'

The whole scene had lasted for less than a minute, but the memory stays with me and even now I replay it in my mind and wonder whether the child survived.

So far on our safari, we had seen many acacia trees (although rather irritatingly the African acacia has recently been reclassified and is now correctly known as Vachellia. I really don't understand why.) However, they can call them whatever they like, but as far as I'm concerned they're acacias. What we hadn't seen until now were the whistling thorn acacias. Now, here they were. Shorter than their cousins, they were decorated with hard, nut-like growths from which the thorns grow, and which are hosts to several varieties of ants who make their homes within them by boring holes. When the wind blows through these holes, the tree whistles. The ants repay their hosts by swarming and stinging browsing animals to deter them from eating the trees' leaves, so it is a symbiotic relationship – housing in return for protection.

Travelling on the rough, rocky, dirt roads to our destination we were several times held up by goats or cattle crossing the road, herded by bands of little dusty children. They ran beside the vehicles, shouting '*Switi, switi!*' What does that mean? I asked Dedan. 'They are asking for sweets.

When they see tourist vehicles coming – they can see the dust a long way off – they drive their animals onto the road so you have to slow down. It is a sweety ambush.'

For these children who do not benefit from dental care, Vivien suggests that a better treat for for them would be pencils or crayons.

We drove on and on, along increasingly spidery tracks that had nothing to distinguish them from spidery tracks we'd already driven on, until we reached a place where the track forked. Dedan shook his head, announcing that he was lost and didn't know whether to take the left or right fork. He chose the right and turned down another spidery path, through a clump of bushes, into in a dusty compound and parked. Just his little joke. He does have a deadpan sense of humour.

Unless you knew exactly where you were going, you wouldn't find this place. There are no signs anywhere for the Little Mara Bush Camp, nor any indication that there's anything here until you reach the car park in a small clearing surrounded by shrubs and trees.

Chapter Twenty-one

SPEAK SWAHILI: LALA SALAMA – SLEEP WELL

When I was growing up in Kenya, my best friend's father was a camping fanatic. He took us to the most remote places, with a gigantic green canvas tent. It weighed tons and took hours to erect. His wife was tiny, and we were two puny 12-year-old girls. We struggled with acres of heavy duty canvas – I think it was an ex-military tent that had probably taken a dozen strapping soldiers to erect – miles of heavy rope, and sacks of hefty wooden pegs that required the strength of Hercules to hammer into the ground. But once it was finally up it was the size of a ballroom. He used a trenching tool to dig a deep pit which was our lavatory, well away from the tent, and we never gave a thought to what wildlife was watching us as we journeyed there and back. We slept on narrow canvas camp beds that were inclined to tip over if we moved; the stars and paraffin lamps were our source of illumination, and we cooked over a small gas stove or an open fire. We tripped over the guy ropes, spent half the night trying to escape mosquitos, and had to bang out our shoes to evict spiders or lurking scorpions. Various creepy crawlies crept and crawled all around us and things snuffled and snorted in the night. Much of our day was spent carrying buckets of water from a river, and collecting firewood. I think my friend's father was a frustrated sergeant major who would have preferred to have had a son to a daughter. I recall him barking orders and making us put our shoulders back and look lively. In retrospect, it was actually a lot of fun, but at the time it seemed like a punishment, and it was always a relief when the tent had been dismantled and crammed back into the trailer, and we headed back to flushing toilets and beds that didn't tip over.

However, the tents in which we would be staying for the next four days in the Mara were something else. For a start, we didn't have to erect them. They were rigid, double-lined, insect-proofed, enormous, and luxurious and firmly planted on wooden raised platforms.

The camp was quite a contrast after the sophisticated accommodation we had so far stayed in. There are no flower beds, no ornamental trees, no swimming pool – just nature, wild and untamed. It's designed to have minimal impact on the environment, with solar panels providing power and a generator in case of need. The tents are discreetly placed among the bushes, far apart from each other to ensure privacy for the occupants. Apart from narrow tracks leading to the tents and the communal buildings, the bush remains untouched. Unique metal animal sculptures identify each tent. We were in the 'hippo and calf' tent. A hundred yards away, there's a tented dining room used in case of inclement weather, but mostly we would eat *al fresco*. The communal lounge has facilities to charge computers and batteries, and download photos. Sophisticated water management systems deal with waste.

Without the landscaped gardens, swimming pool or any permanent buildings, a passer-by might think that there is nothing particularly impressive about the camp. The pathways are narrow squiggles of dust and gravel, and from the outside the large tents just look like tents. However, once you step inside, you enter an opulent world.

Our tent stood right on the bank of the Olare Orok river where the hippos live. It contained two large double bedrooms, a four-poster bed, thick oriental rugs, elegant furniture and netting to keep even the smallest ant outside. There was a proper modern flushing loo, twin onyx wash basins and a shower. There were containers of eco-friendly shampoos and soaps, big fluffy towels, colourful cotton dressing gowns and soft slippers. The main room opened up onto a long wooden verandah where we could sit and watch the hippos plopping around in the water.

The camp is unfenced and animals are free to roam around within it, so Maasai warriors escorted us wherever we walked within the camp. Our guard's name was Muserian, tall, young and shy, with a glorious white smile. He carried a spear and wore a token red tartan *shuka* over trousers, suede boots, a T-shirt and a green military-style sweater topped off with a beanie. He would stand guard all night.

Being so isolated, I asked camp manager Michela about staff facilities, and she told me that employees sleep in an adjacent staff village where they receive three meals a day as well as morning and afternoon tea. Their home villages are usually several hours away, and the camp often transports them there and back. When time permits and the camp is not busy, they take the staff on game drives. It sounded like a dream job. Staff are recruited through recommendation of other trusted staff members. As well as paying a fee for every client to the Maasai who own the land, at least half of the employees come from the local community, and the camp offers free training to assist them in finding work within the tourism sector.

After lunch, Vivien suggested a game of Scrabble. There were a few nervous throat-clearings amongst those who had played with her previously, and they all suddenly had to do something else. Some said they were going to have a rest, some were going to take a shower. Some were catching up with their emails. Some wished to download their photos and recharge their batteries. That only left me, and although it was years since I played I was more than happy to sit on the shaded deck overlooking the pool where the fat creatures live. As we walked down the narrow path from the camp to the deck, a snorting sound coming up fast behind us gave us just sufficient warning to step to one side as a couple of zebras galloped past.

Vivien

Vivien functioned on high-octane tea. Any time she sat down, she ordered a pot of tea. She liked her tea so strong that it felt as if it was stripping the enamel from your teeth, and it had to be served from a pot, with a separate jug of cold milk – *chai ya mzungu* – white man's tea.

With the tea tray settled by her side and the hippos blowing bubbles in the river a few yards away, we picked our tiles and started laying down words. The last time I had played Scrabble, the minimum word length was three letters. It seems the rules have since changed, and two-letter words are permitted. Immediately, Vivien was making high scores with single letters forming words I've never heard of.

'What exactly does that mean?' I asked.

'It's an engineering term,' she replied vaguely.

'But what does it mean?'

'It's just an engineering term,' she repeated, laying down another single letter for a score of 28.

'What is that?' I asked, pointing to the new two-letter word.

'That's an engineering term too.'

In between bouts remarkable for the amount of mysterious two-letter engineering terms deployed, we watched the hippos. They are not especially active or entertaining creatures, because they seem to do nothing but lie beneath the surface with their eyes, ears and nostrils showing, erupting from the water every so often and sploshing noisily for a few seconds before submerging again. When you've seen it two or three times, you've got the idea.

'I'm out!' cried Vivien triumphantly, placing her final tile to make the word 'wid'.

'Well done,' I replied. 'I expect that's an engineering term. We must play again one day.' I heard a snort and giggle from the people who were sitting near us and realised then why everybody else was too busy to play with her.

I didn't go on the afternoon game drive because I needed to organise and wash some of our clothes which were all jumbled up after our frequent moves. With organic washing powder provided by the camp, I worked up the suds, rinsed as sparingly as possible – water is such a precious commodity – and draped the wet things over the rail of the verandah under the eyes of a family of semi-submerged hippos who snorted occasionally and flicked their ears.

Before dinner, we partook of cocktails – jokingly known as '*dawa*', the Swahili word for medicine – while one of the staff passed around trays of exquisite miniature samosas and small cheese pastries, freshly baked by chef Fred. Living in the country famed for its pastries, I can vouch for the fact that those little mouthfuls would hold their own in the most upmarket patisseries anywhere in the world.

We ate at a long communal table beneath the stars and trees. Our starter was a delicate chilled avocado soup served with fragrant bread rolls. There is no high-tech kitchen there: meals are prepared in a tent. A rigid tent, equipped with refrigerators powered by generators, and all the mod cons needed to produce food, but nevertheless a tent. Although the choice was more limited than the lavish buffets we had enjoyed in the 5-star lodges, there was a subtle difference in the food here, it was more personal, you could taste the love in every dish. Chef Fred was from the Samburu tribe, far from his home. Unlike the flamboyant Samburu we had met, Fred was quiet and rather shy. He was delighted when we all complimented him on his cooking and everyone we spoke to agreed that it was the food there that we had most enjoyed on our trip so far.

I was curious as to how Fred managed to prepare sophisticated meals out there, off the beaten track at least 100 miles from the nearest town of any size. The nearest place for even the simplest shopping was a 45-minute drive to the tiny village of Talek. He laughed, explaining that he did all his ordering over the Internet; dry goods were delivered once a month, and fresh food weekly. Thanks to fridges and freezers run by the generator, all the food was kept fresh and safely stored.

Fred really did put his heart and soul into every meal. One of our group, Michael was very health conscious and wherever we stayed, he had to have a daily green smoothie. I'm not sure what all the ingredients were, I think there was kale and ginger and some other healthy stuff. He'd given the recipe to Vivien, who ensured that everywhere we went, the kitchen staff made this special drink for him. Fred liked to put his own twist on it, too. One day the green smoothie was bright red.

We would be up and out by sunrise next day so opted for an early night. Our spear-wielding guard Muserian led the way to our tent by torchlight, and waited patiently while we zipped ourselves in before he began his nocturnal patrol.

As we slid through the mosquito net into our giant four-poster bed, between the cool, white sheets my toes found something warm and furry. I prodded it softly, hoping it wouldn't bite, then peeled back the covers to reveal a fleece-wrapped hot water bottle. The nights do get cool, and this was another example of how the Little Mara Bush camp went the extra mile to ensure comfort for their guests down to the smallest detail.

When I mentioned the hot water bottle next day to Michela she laughed.

'One guest – before my time, but I was told about it – thought it was an animal, and stabbed it.'

I thought how foolish anybody would seem, having a soaking mattress and having to admit to having killed a hot water bottle. Bob said that when he felt it with his feet he thought it was a cat or a monkey, however he didn't consider attacking it. We did love Bob with his air of bewilderment and grumpiness, but in his eyes there was always a gleam of merriment. We had much in common, as he's an Anglophile and enjoyed talking about England, and in particular his partiality to Tiptree jams and crumpets.

The night was full of intriguing sounds. Grunts, squeals, roars, rattles, growls, splashes, crashes, squeaks, chewing and belching. What a heavenly sensation of being so very, very close to nature with nothing more than a wall of thick canvas between us, and knowing at the same time that we were perfectly safe. It gave me a feeling of calm and being in another world.

Chapter Twenty-two

SPEAK SWAHILI: NYOKA – SNAKE

Muserian was waiting outside our tent as we made our way to breakfast. We asked him if any animals had come close during the night.

'Yes,' he smiled, 'lion in the car park, and hippos just here.' He pointed to a trampled patch of grass beside our tent, leading up the bank from the river.

'Aren't you frightened?' I asked.

He laughed. 'Not frightened!' All he has is a spear with a blade at one end and a spike at the other, and a torch.

Later, I ask Michela if there was a contingency plan in place for when a spear and torch proved inadequate. She replied that generally it took nothing more than a bit of noise to encourage the animals to change course, so the watchmen bang pieces of wood together. They all have mobile phones to call for assistance if necessary, and there is an armed guard always ready to intervene to frighten away any unwelcome visitors.

Although they are hunted for meat and are losing their habitat to human encroachment, the hippo is not yet in danger of extinction. With their balloon-like bodies and little stumpy legs they look like amiable cartoon creatures, and not like highly dangerous animals responsible for more human deaths in Africa than any other creature except the mosquito.

Despite their Billy Bunter appearance, they are fast. You couldn't outrun them and you couldn't outswim them. They are territorial, and extremely aggressive towards any real or perceived threat, so if you happen to annoy or startle them or to be in their way when they are in a hurry, they will not go around you. With their immense jaws and giant incisors they can bite a man in half, and with a bodyweight of over 3 tons they can squash you as flat as a carpet. Keep out of their way.

Mainly nocturnal creatures, they spend the daylight hours submerged, clambering out of the water at nightfall to lumber up to twenty miles to graze, returning before dawn to hurl themselves back into the water and adopt the 'butter wouldn't melt in my mouth' appearance, like mischievous schoolboys. They are not great swimmers, but bounce along the river bed on their toes – boing, boing, boing. In the same way that camels are adapted to protect their ears, eyes and noses from sand, the hippo is designed to be able to close off its ears, eyes and nostrils while it's prancing around underwater. Beneath their chins and bellies, and around their ears and eyes, their skin is a pretty shade of pink, as if whoever painted them ran out of grey paint. The pinkness is a natural oily sunscreen that they secrete to protect their surprisingly-delicate skin from sunburn when they are out of the water.

Their toilet habits are uninhibited. While excreting copious quantities of digested plants in a stream of pungent liquid greenery, they simultaneously whisk it up in the water with their little tails, flinging it far and wide and creating a foul-smelling frothy mess which feeds the mudfish that are abundant in the river. I'm probably not going to eat mudfish.

It was our first drive with Steve who, when he wasn't driving, was almost always bent double, slapping his knees and roaring over some joke. Peggy and Tom were our co-passengers, and Peggy gave her head a hefty whack climbing into the Land Cruiser. Any of the other guides would have expressed concern but Steve simply said: 'Don't break my car.' He was a laugh-a-minute man as well as a *bona fide* poacher-turned-gamekeeper. Coming from a poor family, he grew up hunting wildlife for food, until he realised the importance of protecting that wildlife, and decided to become a guide. He is known as Eagle Eye for his unique ability to spot animals and birds invisible to mere mortals.

Steve

We were on the plains before the sun came up, and were rewarded with an almost surreal sky of orange and red framing the perfect silhouette of a lone thorn tree. A short distance from the camp is a shallow river interspersed with smooth shiny rocks that slope at a fairly steep angle. The vehicles have to cross here. The rocks form a natural dam where the green foam produced by the hippos' whisked droppings collect. It looked and smelled 'organic' which is why it is known as Stinky Crossing. We needed to have confidence in the driving skills of our guides because the vehicles were tilted precariously, and a hippo just a few feet away was watching our progress as if it was hoping at least one of us would fall over.

As we came over the crest of the hill at the other side of the crossing, we found a pride of glossy lions in the golden grass, enjoying their breakfast of something no longer identifiable, just a large rib cage. Some of them were eating, the others playing, chasing each other and stopping obligingly to pose, relaxed and confident. Lazing in the sun, they looked as benevolent as domestic cats, as if you could walk up to them and rub them behind their ears, but when a bird landed near the carcass, a lioness was on her feet and springing into the air to chase it off, moving from supine to airborne faster than the eye could follow.

Steve pointed out an animal I didn't recall having ever seen before. Topi are striking antelope, their short coats dark copper in colour with the same burnished metallic sheen as the wildebeeste. Their limbs, from the hips and shoulders down to the hocks and knees are a deep blue-grey colour which is why their nickname is Blue Jean antelope, while the lower part of their limbs is a golden yellow, which coupled with the blue jeans is reminiscent of teenagers wearing yellow stockings under denim shorts.

Their black faces are topped with lyre-shaped, ringed horns. If I had designed them, I would have put their eyes slightly lower down, as they are very high up, just beneath the horns and level with the base of their ears. There's a large pre-orbital gland visible beneath the eye, and another gland on the feet, which they use for territory marking. Typically, they like to stand on the tall red anthills to give themselves a vantage point to look out for danger. As their colouring blends well with the anthills, this pose makes them appear larger to predators.

It was the season when the great migration of the herds takes place, where the animals cross the river from the Serengeti to reach the rich grazing in the Mara triangle, and we drove down to the river to see if there were any signs of activity. On the far bank, a handful of gnus and a few zebra stood around studying the water as if they might venture across, until a tractor coming down to the pumping station disturbed them and they wandered off. Steve pointed out a couple of semi-submerged hippos and two crocodiles sunning themselves on a small sandbank. Like sushi, improvised jazz and Tracey Emin's 'My Bed' I have tried hard, many times, to find some redeeming feature in crocodiles, and failed. We waited a while to see if the animals would begin to cross, and when nothing happened we went away to look for something else.

Steve stopped the vehicle and jumped out.

'What's happening?' we asked.

To our horror he replied, 'I'm going to kill a snake.'

A conservationist killing a reptile was appalling behaviour. There are some highly venomous snakes in Kenya, particularly the black mamba and the puff adder which are both aggressive when cornered, but we were at no risk in the vehicle and could not understand why Steve felt it necessary to get out to kill one. I'd rather gone off him and was wondering how to tell Vivien that one of her guides had gone out of his way to kill a creature that posed no risk to us, because it went against everything that she believed in. This would be the first snake we had even had a chance of seeing.

Peggy and Tom, Terry and myself all called out in alarm:

'Stop!' 'Just leave it!' 'Don't do this!' 'You don't need to kill it!'

'It has to be done,' he shouted back as he marched towards a small bush. Then he turned round with a huge grin. 'Don't worry – I am just going to 'mark my territory''.

As well as being a joker, he is a driving enthusiast whose ambition is to take part in the Rhino Charge, a lunatic annual off-road driving contest to raise funds for rhino conservation and environmental improvements. Entrance fees are high – $100 as well as a minimum sponsorship of $2,000, which for the time being put it beyond his means to participate, but he followed as a spectator.

Ahead of us was a very deep *donga*, a gully with sides that were almost perpendicular, and he was looking at it longingly, torn between wanting to have a go and the responsibility of not getting his passengers stuck in it. His professionalism won, and reluctantly he drove away to another stretch of river to see whether there was any sign of an imminent crossing.

On the opposite bank, a herd of about 200 wildebeeste were milling around. Two dozen zebras stood drinking, fetlock-deep, watched by a lone topi. The crocodiles had moved from the sandbank and were floating around midstream like logs, and a solitary elephant who had been standing up to its belly in the water emerged and clambered up the bank. He walked a few meters and then showered himself with clouds of red dust to apply his sunscreen protection. Having drunk their fill, the zebras turned back, except for one who, seemingly unaware of or unconcerned by the crocodiles, sauntered casually across the river. After standing on the bank looking uncertain and clutching their towels for ten minutes or so, the wildebeeste finally followed, stepping down and bobbing their heads as they plodded slowly through the water, which reached up to their elbows. I could barely manage to watch, so worried that something would be injured. Even in the relatively shallow water, the youngest and weakest animals struggled, but they all reached the far side safely and moved off onto the plains, grunting, mooing and honking, their grey bodies glistening with water.

When it was clear that nothing else was going to happen, we drove away, stopping to watch a secretary bird strutting by in the long grass, 4 feet of regal self-importance. I'd always understood that it got its name from the quill features that form its crest, making it appear to have a collection of pencils stuck behind its (non-existent) ears. However, Steve said that it is a derivation of the Arabic '*saqr-et-tair*', meaning 'hunter bird'. They are adept snake killers, and also eat insects and small mammals. As big as it was, it was dwarfed by an even larger black and white saddle-billed stork, which has the body of a giant magpie, enormously long legs and a huge black and red bill that bears a striking yellow 'saddle' at the top.

The sun had vanished and the skies were dark. A few drops of rain fell, and a rainbow formed against the grey clouds. Half a dozen vehicles were parked up in the distance, and as we joined them we saw that the rainbow was framing a magnificent male lion sitting in the long grass, his great bouffant mane tousled by the wind, his nose in the air and eyes closed as if he was enjoying the breeze on his face.

Steve edged a couple of metres closer to the lion, who turned one sleepy eye towards us and then closed it again. We sat there watching him for five minutes, until there was a flurry of activity, engines starting, and we were driving away, but not fast enough to avoid the Park Rangers who signalled Steve to stop. There are stringent regulations in the park regarding keeping to the roads and it is one of the responsibilities of the Park Rangers to enforce the rules. They talked with Steve, saying that he had been seen parked off the road. Their conversation was amicable, and I heard him saying that he was on the '*bura bura wa samani*' – the old road. Telling him to stay where he was, the rangers went to examine the wheel tracks which were clearly visible after the rain. They returned and agreed that he was on the old road that ran parallel to the new one, and although he shouldn't have been, they would let him off this time. Word had quickly spread to other guides, and as we drove back to camp, vehicles pulled up alongside to slap hands with Steve, with lots of laughs and congratulations. He was the man of the moment. The guides are all dedicated conservationists, committed to the welfare of all wildlife and would do nothing to cause them stress or harm.

When Terry had insisted on bringing his laptop with us, I had thought it would be an unnecessary encumbrance. Having divested ourselves of bulky DSLR cameras and huge lenses in favour of our compact Olympus OMDs, surely carrying a computer would be defeating the object of travelling light? However, without it we would have been in a mess, because I had not foreseen the number of photographs we would be taking every day. Our cameras were clicking non-stop, our SD cards quickly filling up, so we needed to download them regularly, which was my job at the end of each day. Back at the camp that evening, I settled down with the computer. The keyboard was gritty with dust so I took a cloth and swiped it over a few times. The alarming result was that the monitor display turned itself upside down, and I couldn't find any way of returning it to its rightful position. The mouse travelled haphazardly all over the place, and it was impossible to manipulate it because it went in the opposite direction to where I aimed it, and even if I tried to point it opposite to where I wanted it, it still went where it chose.

Why on earth would it even be possible to turn a monitor upside down? Who would want to do that?

Luckily, the beautiful, eternally-smiling Jessica stepped in. She's an IT wizard, one of a small number of female software engineers from the 1980s, and was confident that between the two of us we could solve the problem. Privately, I was thinking it was unsolvable, but Jessica asked me to have faith in her, so I did. With much giggling, a little cursing, and me standing behind the monitor and craning my face downwards, I was able to direct the mouse to where she pointed with her finger, and thus she managed to get into the computer's settings and from there into the graphics properties and get the screen the right way up. I'm still wondering at the logic behind it.

After dinner that evening, we sat in a circle around a camp fire, African television style, and Vivien entertained us with stories of her adventures in Kenya. Whatever she is involved in she gives it all her enormous energy, passion and positivity. I'd never heard a negative word from her – almost to the point of finding it irritating, sometimes. Any objection or doubt she simply brushes away like a tiresome fly. 'There's no time for that nonsense,' she'd say. 'Let's just get on and do it.' For her there were never problems, only situations to deal with. She's one of the most inspirational people I know, and one of the most modest, and it is very, very unusual to hear her talk about any of her achievements.

It was Bob's wife, quiet, gentle Beth who persuaded her to tell us more about herself. Our travelling companions of the 95th Memorial group had only previously known Vivien socially, and I don't think any of them had any idea of her 'other' life as a bossy, dynamic perfectionist.

Beth asked Vivien how she had become involved in the safari business.

'Well,' she began, 'I had been living in the USA with my husband at the time, and we had sold our house, and not yet purchased another. He suggested I go to Kenya for a year with our daughter whilst he kept looking for another house on the West Coast of the USA, and he would commute. There was a loophole in the law which said, 'If one spouse lives and works abroad, you can delay the paying of capital gains tax.'

She followed his suggestion and moved back to Kenya. Having been out of the job market for twelve years it was difficult to get back in, but she was offered an opportunity to work with a local safari company, which she did for several years until she was introduced to the legendary former white hunter, Brian Nicholson. He had been Senior Game Warden in Tanzania for 24 years, and had mapped the Selous Game

Reserve, the largest uninhabited park in the world. He had unequalled experience in active elephant control operations and dealing with man-eating lions. An outstanding bushman and guide, he had travelled thousands of miles on foot with porters. When he came to her one day and asked if she knew a caterer, as he had a group of 15 schoolteachers coming to his camp in the Maasai Mara for Christmas, Vivien immediately volunteered. Nicholson asked, 'Can you cook?' She replied: 'Yes, Brian, I can cook, but some things I will have to make ahead, like the Christmas pudding and cake.'

When she arrived at Nicholson's old hunter-style camp, she found the 'kitchen' comprised of a tarpaulin held up by four posts, with wilderness all around. The stove was an oblong of stones filled with ashes with an iron grate across the top on which the pots could sit. The coals to make the fire were thrust under the grate from a fire burning to the side of the kitchen.

Although the Christmas festivities and food all required some ingenuity, decorations being made out of foil and a few twigs, there was a full Christmas meal of roast turkey, ham, stuffing and all the trimmings, followed by Christmas pudding, brandy butter and custard, and plenty of Christmas cake and mince pies to last over several days. After the teachers left, Brian received a message saying that they had their school Christmas meal at the Savoy hotel in London, but the food they had in the camp was so much better! From that day on, Vivien became the caterer for Nicholson's camp, where Kamara also worked and where his association with Vivien began.

Beth asked whether she had ever had any frightening moments. Despite her tiny size, she is absolutely fearless, with the heart of a lion, so I was particularly interested to hear her reply.

On her first day at the camp, she found that next to the 'kitchen' in the glaring sun was a very hot tent in which there was a refrigerator, and where all the fresh vegetables were laid out on sacks on the floor, the beans and leeks curling up at the edges. Nearby in the shade was another tent, in which there was a pile of potatoes, some broken chairs and crates of sodas. Vivien decided to switch the contents of the tents around so the refrigerator and the fresh produce could be in the shade.

Next morning while Brian and Kamara were collecting the teachers from the airstrip, she summoned two men to help her move the refrigerator. As she was bending over in the corner near the potatoes, she saw something moving right under her hand. As she looked closer a large head and eyes appeared less than a foot from her face.

'Forget the Olympics,' Vivien laughed, 'you should have seen this kid move!'

She ran out of the tent as fast as she could, yelling, '*Nyoka, nyoka!*' The two men helping her were also running frantically.

Vivien asked them: 'Why are you running?'

'Because you are running, Mama!'

They went back to the tent where they found a huge puff adder. For those who don't know, this is a particularly unattractive snake. It doesn't share the lithe elegance of the mambas, the arrogant pride of the cobra, or the sleekness of the python. It is a big floppy snake that looks as if somebody let out some of the air, so it has a sort of collapsed-looking body. If disturbed, it is extremely bad-tempered, and can transform from a sluggish squashed-looking coil into a rapidly-striking set of lethal fangs.

Listening to her talking, I suspected that I was the only person there who knew what her reaction would have been: save the snake! To her all life is sacrosanct.

She wanted it put into a sack or box so it could be driven and released far away from human habitat, but being the rookie at the camp she was overruled by the staff, who said they had to kill it before the clients arrived. Had she been more experienced she would never have allowed it to happen, but that time the poor snake, who had not harmed her, was killed. She was still upset when she remembered that incident which was nearly 30 years ago.

I rather like snakes and was always on the look out for a sighting, but during the 17 days we spent in the reserves, I never saw one.

The fire was dying down, the embers pulsing lazily, sparks jumping and fizzling out, and the ashes fluttering in a warm breeze. The stars were low enough to touch, and the sky inky black.

'Tell us more about your adventures there,' we urged.

Once, she said, she was called to the staff tents to see Onyego, one of the camp workers. He was lying flat in bed with terrible chest pains. Vivien took his temperature which was very high, and she was afraid that he was having a heart attack. He needed to be taken to hospital as soon as possible, but all the safari vehicles were out on game drives, and Kamara had taken the truck to fill the water drums. The only way she could summon help was via the camp radio attached to a tree on the top of a steep hill nearby. She called Air Kenya who said they could only fly the sick man out if he had a doctor's certificate. She said she would get it and bring him to the airstrip for the 4pm flight to Nairobi.

The doctor was at his clinic at least 6 miles away, and with no vehicles available there was only one thing for it. Walk and walk fast. So she set off with Rashid the chef, who carried a spear for protection. They walked up hills, down hills, through the forest and across the plains until they reached the clinic, where the doctor gave them the necessary certificate. Then they hurried back the way they came. When they reached the camp, Kamara had returned with the truck and he drove the sick man to the airstrip with his doctor's certificate. Onyego was flown to Nairobi and transferred to the Nairobi Hospital with lighting speed, where he was successfully treated. He has remained a loyal friend to Vivien.

In 1997, with years of safari experience under her belt she started her own company, *As You Like it (Safaris) Ltd.*

She had got into her stride now, and we were all captivated. Go on, we said, tell us more.

'Well, let me see. Oh, yes, there was the time when I was in my house in Karen, a suburb of Nairobi. In the middle of the night, someone was banging on the door, then on the window, calling me anxiously. I shouted out of the window to ask what was happening. It was the gardener, Symon, who said that his wife was having a baby and needed help. There was no time to send for medical help, nor to drive to a hospital, so I had to do something. I was used to delivering puppies and foals, so I ran around in a few circles like a dog before it pees, and filled a bucket with hot water, grabbed a bottle of disinfectant, towels, some fine string. The woman was squatting, her waters had just broken. I asked if it was her due date, but no, it was not, this was going to be a premature baby.

'When the baby's head popped out, I grabbed it with towels. Then I knew I was meant to do something about the umbilical cord. Using my experience with puppies when their mother didn't sever the cord for them, I took the string and tied the cord close to the infant's stomach. I debated whether I ought to hold the baby upside down and make it cry, but as it was premature I kept it wrapped in towels, cleared its nostrils and told the mother to go and wash herself. Then I handed the baby to Symon and collected together underwear and sanitary pads. By then it was 2am, and I drove as fast as I could to Kenyatta National Hospital, where I rushed in with the baby and told them it needed attention right away. Mother and child were quickly whisked away, and after a long wait the doctor came to say I had done a great job, and took me to see the baby in an incubator. At 4am, Symon and I were driving home, thrilled and elated.'

She didn't mention that during the war in Iraq she had worked as a civilian in Baghdad, employed as an Administrator by an American company contracted by USIS to run a Special Forces Police Training Camp for the Iraqis. During that time, after unwanted attention she told the men in her office that she wanted to be seen with a gun and know how to use it. She spent an afternoon at the firing range, where she learned to handle several different guns. The AK47 was the best, she had told me with a grin.

Listening to her I was envious, thinking how very mundane my own life has been in contrast, although if I'm honest I doubt I could have done half of what she has. She has superhuman energy and is driven to perfection. She was always first up in the morning, last to bed at night, checking and rechecking that everybody was happy and everything was in order. Which meant that we had absolutely nothing to do except relax and enjoy ourselves and no decisions to take apart from choosing what to eat. Bliss.

Chapter Twenty-three

SPEAK SWAHILI: TOTO – CHILD

Although I had abysmally failed to adapt to getting up in what seemed like the middle of the night, the horror was softened at the Little Mara Bush Camp by the quiet voice that called 'Good morning.' One of the staff arrived each day with a fragrant cafetière of coffee and plate of small pastries which he placed on the writing desk and withdrew. While I tended to moan and wail and stumble about, Terry was great at jumping out of bed, humming and bouncing around and when I had finally surfaced, he would be sitting on the verandah with his coffee, listening to the sounds of the night and the occasional burp or snort from the river. Ten minutes of that and I too was ready to rock and roll.

As Muserian escorted us from our tent, there were swallows in the air, dipping and diving as they snatched invisible insects. 'Good sign,' he pointed to the birds. 'Rain coming.'

We were out again with Steve, and Michael who had to have the green smoothie every day. Down at Stinky Crossing, a couple of topi were playing on the bank, their coats gleaming like polished copper in the golden early morning as they chased each other around, tossing their heads and running in circles, carefree and full of *joie de vivre.*

As we edged through Stinky Crossing tilted at a gravity-defying angle, I pointed to the thick green scum of hippo faeces collecting against the bank.

'Look, Michael – that's where your green smoothie comes from!'

'Holy crap!' he laughed.

At the other side of Stinky Crossing, a male lion was stirring in the grass. He stood up as we approached, yawning, stretching and slowly strolling towards the river. We turned back to follow him, and as we reached the crossing, I looked across and could see only one topi, standing on the skyline looking down upon the river bed. I turned to where it was looking. There was the lion hauling a large body away up the bank – one topi would not play again in the early morning light. Lions have a powerful sense of smell and acute hearing, so despite its apparently casual attitude it had most likely scented its prey and knew exactly what it was going to do.

The lion dragged the body away, stopping several times – a full grown topi can weigh more than 300lbs – until it had vanished from sight into a copse of bushes. This I could cope with. I was sad for the animal that had been so full of life, but I knew it had a quick death, and now the lion would feed. Twelve minutes had passed since we had seen the topi playing – I took the data from the EXIF on my camera.

A little further up the stream, a yellow-billed stork stared intently into the water as it paddled methodically, to stir up the small unfortunate creatures below the surface, and stabbing at them with its huge bill.

I saw eland for the first time – magnificent animals, tawny grey/gold in colour, grazing with a herd of zebra and impala. The eland bulls are heavily built with long spearlike horns, dangling dewlaps and a hump on their shoulders similar to Brahma cattle. Despite their great size – eland are the largest of the antelope – they are agile, able to jump high and zigzag to escape predators.

Steve pulled up and switched off the engine, pointing over to our right where fifty yards away a pair of lions were lying in the grass.

'Watch!', he said, 'You are going to see something

special.' The male was in his prime, with a great black mane. Beside him, the lioness was lying on her back with her legs in the air like a strumpet.

'This couple are on honeymoon,' he added. He explained the rules of courtship amongst lions. While a pride may contain several males, it is only the dominant one who will mate with the females. However, it is the lioness who lays down the rules, and when she comes into heat, she flirts, tempting and teasing the male for a couple of days. When she has his full attention, the couple leave the herd to find a place for their honeymoon, and by the third and fourth days they are mating regularly about every 15 minutes. It is a short-lived event, but repeated frequently. After each mating, the lioness lies on her back to ensure that none of the male's efforts are wasted. She will normally conceive on the fourth or fifth day, and once she has done so their love-making becomes uncomfortable. By the sixth or seventh days, they are both tired and hungry. The honeymoon is over, and they rejoin the pride. One hundred and ten days later the cubs will be born.

We sat patiently for 10 minutes at a discreet distance to allow them some privacy, but they were so completely wrapped up in each other they seemed unaware of our presence.

Steve's phone rang, with news that a crossing was about to take place, so we left the lions to their loving and drove to the river. As we reached it, a mini-bus with eight people squashed into it tried to push us off the path. It was both rude and foolish, because Steve didn't have any plans to be pushed off the path, and in a manoeuvre so daring that, for a moment, I expected to tumble into the river, he swerved around the mini-bus and positioned it neatly behind us. Every driver wants to get his passengers to the best possible position – that is how they earn their living, by keeping their clients satisfied. Nevertheless, bad manners is bad protocol and the mini-bus driver looked rather foolish. With a little courtesy, he could have parked comfortably and left room for us beside him. Instead, his passengers were left looking at the broadside of our vehicle.

A herd of 100 or so wildebeeste were preparing to take the plunge, and we could sense their nervous excitement as they milled around. Half the herd were at the edge of the water, the other half perched on a steep high bank. A couple of zebras stepped into the water and began to wade across followed by the rest of the animals. They had a choice: a shallow incline from which they could walk into the water, or a steep bank which required them to leap and plunge. Why some of them chose the latter more demanding route, who knows, but it did make for a very dramatic scene.

The hippos were still floating about, and the crocodiles were basking on the bank as the whole herd negotiated the crossing safely and loped up the other side, mooing happily. I breathed a little sigh of relief as they started to graze. As well as crocodiles, the crush of bodies and the risk of drowning, submerged rocks and stones are also a hazard to the animals, because when the water level is low the animals use them as stepping stones, but they are slippery and a foot can easily become trapped. Then there is no escape.

With perfect timing, the much-needed rain came just as we returned to camp. Muserian had been right about the swallows. The downpour stirred up something which I had always loved and long missed – the vaguely metallic smell that is released when heavy rain hits the dust. I've never smelt it anywhere else.

The shower was heavy but short-lived, and we were able to eat outside. Fred had prepared an authentic African meal for us, cooked *al fresco* in traditional pots and pans over charcoal fires. We ate by the light of the fire, salads, soup, roasted vegetables, *ugali*, and *sukuma wiki* for us, while the carnivores enjoyed a selection of *nyama choma* – roast meats.

Without warning, a band of warriors sprang out from the bushes and ran towards us with a blood-freezing noise, waving spears and yelling. One of them had his spear pointed at Deb, who for a moment looked as if she might fall off her chair. It did give us all rather a shock for a few seconds until we recognised that it was simply the evening's entertainment. The warriors were all the Maasai camp staff in traditional costumes, dancing and singing for us. Like Samburu dancing, Maasai dancing involves a great deal of high jumping on the spot. They make it look effortless, but you have to try this for yourself to see just how hard it is.

After dinner, we persuaded Vivien to give us another tale. I know that she really doesn't enjoy talking about herself and her achievements, but on the other hand she was committed to entertaining us, and like the perfect hostess she settled down by the fire to share one of her experiences as a licensed amateur lady rider.

It was our mutual love of horses that had forged our friendship. She was a far more talented and braver rider than me and used to jump my little grey mare, Cinderella. Since then, she had gone on with two of her own horses to become a highly successful showjumper, but had then moved from showjumping to riding races. I asked why.

She was a member and official of the Jockey Club of Kenya, licensed as a judge and clerk of the scales, a racing correspondent writing articles in the press, and involved in marketing and sponsorship. But, she said, the thrill of winning a race was her greatest joy. She has been a racehorse owner, trainer and winner of dozens of races, but when she was asked to ride in the Nairobi Town Plate – an amateur ladies' horse race – at two days notice and 56 years of age – she hadn't been in the saddle for months, let alone ridden a race. Riding a racehorse is no easy thing. It requires supreme fitness, enormous courage, regular training and a touch of madness. She was not fit and hadn't been training. A less impetuous person would have recognised immediately that it was an impossible task. Still, she has never flunked a challenge, so naturally she agreed, having two of the necessary requisites – courage and madness. During the 48 hours prior to the race she spent hours running up and down stairs to get fit and lose sufficient weight.

On the day of the race she was chucked up into the racing saddle, upon a racehorse on its toes and ready to run, and led into the stalls. At the start she was left behind and the rest of the field quickly began to vanish from sight. Vivien was clinging on to anything that could be clung onto, concentrating only on staying in the tiny saddle. The field were moving further and further ahead as she kept her horse inside on the rails, the shortest distance on the course. On the horizon, she could just the heels and tails of the other horses. Gradually, she began to make up ground, still clinging on like a monkey, and now her competitive nature began to overcome her caution, and she urged the horse onwards. Yard by yard, she moved closer. From the stands, she could hear the African crowd cheering her on.

'Come on *Shushu*!' *Shushu* is the Swahili word for grandmother.

'Come on Granny!'

Shushu pushed, and spoke to her horse, urging it forwards. 'We can do this,' she told it, 'we can win!'

And, of course, they did. That's Vivien in a nutshell.

It was a noisy night. The hippos were behaving like naughty children. We could hear them snorting and puffing as they scrambled up the steep bank and wandered around outside the tent, snuffling as they tore up the grass. There was also a long, low moo followed by a brief yip, and what sounded as if somebody was repeatedly zipping and unzipping their tent. That noise went on for a long time and became very irritating. I couldn't imagine that any members of our group would be standing fiddling with a zip in the middle of the night. Nobody was going to be foolhardy enough to go outside, and as the tents were equipped with luxurious bathrooms and proper flushing lavatories they had no need to. I jammed my fingers in my ears and felt rather grumpy.

Chapter Twenty-four

SPEAK SWAHILI: MARIDADI – PRETTY

Next morning, I asked Muserian about the moo-yip noise.

'Hyena,' he replied.

And which tent was making that zip noise?

He looked blank. 'Nobody was doing that,' he said.

What animals were around the camp last night, we asked?

'Hippo there,' he pointed to the flattened grass right outside our tent.

'Elephant there,' he pointed to some branches lying on the ground.

'Leopard over there,' he pointed across the river.

I mentioned the irritating zip noise to Vivien and asked if she could investigate discreetly and have a word with the zipper.

She laughed. 'That was a leopard,' she said. 'It's one of the noises they make, it sounds like somebody sawing wood.'

Kamara was our guide for the day, and we were sharing a vehicle with Jill, a *pro bono* lawyer and Deb, her retired teacher mother who worked with learning disability children.

Our first sighting was a huge bull elephant that Kamara estimated to be at least 60 years old. It strolled past, almost within arm's reach, as if we were too insignificant to warrant its attention.

The scene on the plains was surreal, as the numbers of wildebeeste had multiplied like popcorn. Tens of thousands of them dotted the grassland and moved across the plains like a giant mower. You could trace their route by the height of the grass – where the previous day it had been waist-high it was now only ankle-deep. Those vast horizons are what I have always missed. Where we live in France you can see for a long way, but nothing in comparison to this. The Kenyan landscape is another world entirely. As Michael put it so well: everywhere you go you can see forever.

Jill was a good spotter, and pointed at a tawny eagle as it swooped to try to snatch a Thomson's gazelle. I was pleased to see the animal fighting back, twisting and turning to face and successfully chase away the bird.

Some of the sights we saw were so unexpected. You could never tell how an encounter would turn out. Just ahead of us, a lioness was slinking through the grass, her movement barely discernible as she moved inch by inch towards a plump warthog that was rooting around in the earth with its back to her, apparently unaware that it was in danger. The lioness crouched and sprang forward to start her run. At the same moment, the warthog turned and rushed straight towards her. Their poor eyesight is compensated with acute hearing and smell. Equipped with four fearsome tusks, its fat little body and stumpy legs can move surprisingly quickly and hit a top speed of around 30 mph. The lioness stopped in her tracks, flicked her tail and strolled away, while the warthog added further insult by trotting around quite close behind as if it was thumbing its nose at her. The battle between predator and prey isn't all one-sided.

I asked Kamara how he had become a guide, and he told us that he had started out as a kitchen boy with Brian Nicholson, then worked his way up to becoming a mechanic, driver, and spotter. When Brian eventually retired and sold his camp to Vivien, Kamara and Vivien continued to work together, with Kamara becoming a driver/guide in his own right, a man who learned his unique skills from the master of them all. Vivien had rewarded his years of loyalty by making him a Director of *As You Like it (Safaris) Ltd.*

With his soft slow speech and calm, avuncular nature, you may have been thinking that Kamara would never do anything to surprise you. But don't be taken in by him – he has an unexpected side that he unleashed when we arrived at the steep *donga* that we had persuaded Steve not to attempt the previous day. Instead of driving past, without warning Kamara turned the steering wheel and accelerated straight down the almost perpendicular incline. Predictably, we were unable to ascend the other equally perpendicular opposite side despite his best efforts, and after some minutes rocking to and fro, he managed to reverse up the way we had come, demonstrating that he has some pretty nifty driving skills.

While we got up early enough each day, gently woken by staff to dress and breakfast at our leisure, our guides had to be up well before us because they too had to wash and dress, breakfast and then ensure their vehicles were waiting and ready to roll as soon as we were. That meant tyres, suspension, water and oil levels checked. Beanbags aboard for the cameras, shukas to cover us from dust and cold if needed, a plentiful supply of bottled water in the chillers, sweets and biscuits topped up and any necessary repairs done. Each morning the vehicles were bright, shiny and spotless. The guides drove us seven days a week from 6.00am to noon, and again from 4.00pm to 6.30pm, and even longer if we were on a long day drive to a new location. It was the eleventh day of our trip and they hadn't had a break. They drove in difficult conditions on primitive roads, constantly spotting game, making certain that they got us close to it – as well as ensuring it was safe to do so – and answering questions. Sometimes I noticed them easing their backs, stretching their fingers, flexing their hands, but if you asked if they were tired, the answer was always 'No, I am not tired.'

I thought of the many hundreds of times they had driven the same routes, answered the same questions, seen the same sights, and yet I never saw or heard any of them express anything other than enthusiasm for their job. It is their job, of course, it's how they earn their living, pay for their families' food and education, but there was never the least hint that they were less than enjoying our company and their work.

Kamara has an almost mystical ability to know where to be, just a little before everybody else has worked it out, which is why we were the first vehicle at the river that morning. The bank was a heaving mass of zebra and wildebeeste milling around beside us, braying and lowing and stamping their feet. It reminded me of shoppers on Black Friday. Although they show no imminent sign of going down into the river, the growing excitement among the animals was tangible. A few more vehicles arrived and lined up along the bank.

We sat for ten minutes or so while a steady stream of animals arrived to join the herds.

'Do you ever get bored, Kamara?' I asked. 'You must have seen all these things so many times before.'

'Never get bored watching animals,' he replied. 'Never get bored. Just relaxed.'

Further along the bank a crocodile lay, sinister, menacing, still as a rock.

My award for the most *outré* conversation of our trip goes to mother and daughter, Deb and Jill. We were waiting quietly for the animals to start crossing the river, and Jill broke the silence.

'Mom,' she said. 'When you die, can I have your gold teeth to make a bracelet?'

'Sure you can,' replied Deb.

These two were always full of fun, always laughing and making me laugh.

Beside us, a zebra walked down to the water's edge, and drank. A dozen others followed and then they began to walk across the river. The wildebeeste followed, slowly at first, in an orderly manner, and then in a seemingly endless stream like liquid poured from a bottle, gathering pace, galloping down the bank, plunging into the water – the river was deep after the rain – and following the zebra. A couple of topi joined them.

On the bank, the crocodile began to move. It snaked itself from side to side, and slithered into the water.

The herds were now thrashing through the river. Some had already reached the other side and were galloping up the bank, onto the red dust and away into the long grass. The noise of splashing water and bleating animals was deafening. Some wildebeeste turned and crossed back, as if they were uncertain which way they were meant to be going. I understood that, it frequently happens to me. The migration is not an annual event, but a continuous cycle of more than a million animals moving back and forwards, following the grazing, and while some may be heading west into the Serengeti in Tanzania, at the same time there are others crossing over into the Masai Mara. But this is the time of year when the mass river crossings take place.

The crocodile had disappeared.

The herds continued to pour down the bank and swim frantically. You could sense their growing panic and see the rolling whites of their eyes.

The crocodile reappeared, its snout and spine visible, swimming straight and fast towards the animals.

'Oh no!' Deb cried.

We watched anxiously. I looked the other way, watching those who had made the crossing safely.

Deb and Jill were becoming increasingly alarmed. I had been taking a video, and kept it trained away from the swimmers.

It was inevitable. From the voices around me, I knew what had happened. One young wildebeeste hadn't made the crossing.

From the far bank, a zebra faced back towards us, calling anxiously. Their call is similar to young puppies barking. The rest of the herd was moving away, but that one stood and kept calling to those still clustered on our side. Over the general hubbub, there was an answering cry. They continued calling to each other for a long time, while we sat watching hundreds more animals getting across safely. Then the zebra trotted down the bank and into the water, swimming across to rejoin the herd on our side. She had come back for her child, and led it away back across the river.

Crossing the Mara

What an emotional scene it had been. Fear, tragedy, victory and relief, all churning around. I felt quite drained, and turned away to find within five yards of our vehicle four very large elephants, just standing there behind us, staring at the river as if they were watching a particularly interesting film. When all the animals had gone, they wandered off.

Later, we were rewarded with a sighting of a large family of mongooses playing and some African wattled lapwings with their startling yellow legs.

In the distance, we could see the rest of our group parked

up beneath a solitary mchunju tree, or desert date tree, and we drove over to see what they had found. It was not at all what we expected.

Together with the camp staff, Vivien had organized a surprise sundowner. Our fellow travellers were standing at long tables set with bottles of wine, soft drinks and snacks.

The sun collapsed in a fiery blaze of colour as we celebrated having witnessed one of the most dramatic and moving events in the world of nature, and new friendships. David has a very good voice, and led Vivien and the guides in a great rendition of the happy Kenyan song, putting his own spin on it. It was a time to dance (my trousers slipping down as usual), to sing, and to be at peace in this beautiful country.

Jambo Bwana, Jambo, Jambo bwana,
Habari gani, Mzuri sana.
Wageni, Wakaribishwa,
Kenya yetu Hakuna Matata.
Kenya nchi nzuri, Hakuna Matata.
Nchi ya maajabu, Hakuna Matata.
Nchi yenye amani, Hakuna Matata.
Hakuna Matata, Hakuna Matata.
Watu wote, Hakuna Matata,
Wakaribishwa, Hakuna Matata.
Hakuna Matata, Hakuna Matata

Hello, Hello, Hello sir,
How are you? I'm very fine
Visitors are welcome to our Kenya
Don't worry. Kenya is a nice country
Don't worry. A country of wonder
Don't worry. A country of peace
Don't worry. Don't worry. Don't worry
Everybody. Don't worry

You're all welcome. Don't worry
Don't worry. Don't worry

The words are simple and what they say is true: Kenya is not just a nice country, it is a fabulous country, it is a wondrous country, and a peaceful country. Visitors are welcome and treated with respect and friendship.

A few days ago, it had felt as if we would be there forever, but I recognised with a pang that time was running out and this was the beginning of 'Goodbye.' In two days' time, we would be leaving the Mara to return to Nairobi, and then home.

Our final sight as we drove back to camp was of two ostriches courting. It was an intricate, stylised performance, like watching a scene from the court of Henry VIII, with much curtseying, bowing, bobbing, spreading of the wings, walking stately circles, fluttering of fans and come-hither looks.

After a final dinner cooked by the ever-smiling Fred and his team, I reluctantly packed, ready to leave next morning. Out here in the middle of the African bush, we had been treated like royalty. We were going to miss being awakened at hour eleven and a half of the night by that soft voice calling 'Good morning,' bringing that fragrant pot of coffee and assortment of tiny, fresh-baked cakes for us to sit and sip and nibble on the deck, listening to the snorting of the hippos as the night sky faded slowly towards dawn.

We'd become used to seeing Muserian's smiling face waiting on the path for us as we emerged from the tent. We'd become used to breakfasting in the cool of the morning, on fresh fruit and cereals, full cooked English breakfast and bread rolls still warm from the oven. We were going to miss eating our meals *al fresco*, and we were going to miss Little Mara Bush camp and their friendly, thoughtful staff so very much.

The camp had given us the very best of both worlds – luxury and comfort with an authentic back-to-nature feel. It had been so good for the soul to walk where there was no tarmac, no street lighting, no fences, to feel close to the earth.

I didn't sleep very much, but simply lay there soaking up the sounds of the African night to embed them into my memory.

As if to bid us farewell, the hyenas giggled, the leopard made the zip noise, the hippos splashed and grunted, and we could hear the bushes cracking and the 'stomach rumbling' noises that elephants use to communicate. They were very, very close.

Before we left the following morning, while we were tipping the staff, Fred gave me a handwritten copy of the recipe for the avocado soup that we had all enjoyed so much.

Here it is:

Blend or mash some ripe avocados, but don't blend them too fine. Leave a few small lumps. Add enough cold milk to give a creamy consistency, salt and pepper, and Worcester sauce to taste. Chill in the fridge for 3 hours, and serve cold.

How simple, and simply delicious. Try it.

Chapter Twenty-five

SPEAK SWAHILI: MZUNGU – WHITE MAN

Although we were leaving the Little Mara Bush Camp, we were not leaving the Masai Mara reserve for another couple of days, but moving to the five star Mara Serena Safari Lodge. For some reason that I didn't understand – possibly to do with a river crossing being too flooded – to move to our next location, we had to drive out of the reserve and over the Tanzanian border, then from there cross back into Kenya and back into the reserve.

We were riding with Dedan who was leading the convoy. En route, his eyes were constantly scanning the plains, so when he pulled over and switched off the engine we asked why. He gazed over to our left where we could see nothing.

'Is there something there?' we asked.

'There is something there,' he replied. 'You just have to look.'

It took a few seconds before we spotted a cheetah 30 yards away, lying perfectly camouflaged in the grass. Four small babies peered at us over her back with their tear-stained, slightly indignant little faces. After a while they gained confidence and began to move around, wandering a few yards away and then scampering back to climb on her and tug at her ears. At 6 or 8 weeks old, their coats were greyish and fluffy, with spots showing clearly on their legs and faintly on their bellies, with long pale grey hair running from between their ears to the base of their tails. These babies were hyperactive, wrestling with each other and exploring further and further afield while their mother lay in the grass, keeping one eye on them and the other on a herd of Grant's gazelles grazing nearby.

Each time it seemed the cubs were finally going to settle down, one of them jumped up and bounded off, or bit its mother's ears. She was incredibly patient, until at last all four curled up in a heap and fell asleep. She sat up slowly and studied the gazelles. Moving almost imperceptibly, she rose to her feet, and with lowered head walked a few paces forward, freezing every few seconds. The gazelles grazed peacefully as she slunk closer until she was almost within striking distance. Just as it seemed inevitable that she would make a kill and I was getting ready to look away, mother's four little helpers sat up, saw that she had moved away, and bounded merrily over to her. The herd turned and stared at her, and casually moved away. Knowing that she had been seen, she lay down again, once more a motherly playground. Poor mother, how difficult it must be for her to feed her family if they won't let her hunt in peace.

Dedan asked whether cheetahs belong to the cat family or dog family. I remembered many years ago being told that a cheetah did not belong to the cat family, because it cannot retract its claws, making it closer to the dog. However, it seems I was wrong

'No,' he said, 'they are classified as feline for two reasons: Firstly, they purr, and secondly they are retromingent.'

Because we have owned many cats, and having once witnessed a lioness at the Nairobi Animal Orphanage spraying a visitor with a torrent of urine, I did know what that means. The clue is in 'retro'.

'They are what?' asked Terry.

'They pee backwards,' I replied. I think I won that round.

The border crossing was indicated by a cracked concrete pillar that delineates the invisible line between the two countries. That's it, just a mini-pyramid of crumbly concrete with a T for Tanzania painted on the left, and K for Kenya painted on the right. No barrier, no formalities. No people.

We re-entered the Masai Mara reserve through a park gate. It took some time, and while our guides dealt with the formalities we had a chance to stretch our legs. While we were standing counting slumbering hippos on the river bank (there were 24), a vervet monkey had found its way into one of the Land Cruisers and was about to make off with somebody's sunglasses. An agama lizard posed on a rock absorbing the mid-morning sun. With its scarlet head and body joined to its indigo hind quarters and tail, it looked like two different lizards stuck together, and it was so still that I wondered for a moment whether it was real or plastic. It stared unblinking as I walked around photographing it, with only the slight movement of its pulse giving it away.

The Mara Serena Safari Lodge sits on a hill at the centre of the Maasai Mara triangle. From some distance away, there appears to be a cluster of unusually straight trees on the hill which are actually mobile phone masts, decorated with artificial branches to blend in with nature. The track leading to the lodge is lined with cheerful yellow tifonia flowers, and the entrance offers what must be one of the most spectacular views on earth. The parking area leads down into a luminous atrium crowned by a cupola, the walls decorated in soft shades of pastel green and yellow, and directly ahead is a terrace from where you look out to the plains and beyond to the ends of the earth.

It does something to you, this infinite space, so tranquil on the surface, yet so teeming with life. You feel at once insignificant and amazing, just for being here. I wanted to hold out my arms and gather it all in, hold it pressed to my heart, never let it go. I wanted to lay it softly between sheets of tissue and put it in a drawer to be brought out and stroked every day. I wanted to bottle it in a crystal jar and place it on a sunny windowsill to be forever in my sight. This magnificent, beautiful country, birthplace of mankind, owner of my heart.

Our accommodation at the Mara Serena was in individual bungalows shaped like Maasai huts, blended into the flowering trees and plants where birds and butterflies sang and danced and sunned themselves. The cheerful porter who had heaved our luggage from the car park told us proudly that he had two wives and nine children.

While Terry went to take a shower, I opened the sliding glass door onto our private deck and stood looking out over the plains, then turned to the writing desk to pick up a new camera battery. A flash of movement caught my eye and I looked around to find myself face to face with a very large baboon that had come in through the doors and was casing the joint with its sharp eyes.

'Hello,' I said. 'What can I do for you?' It flashed me a peeved look and vaulted over the verandah.

'Who were you talking to?' Terry called from the bathroom.

'A baboon, it came in from the deck.'

'What? I can't hear you.'

I stepped closer to the bathroom, and immediately our visitor was back, on the table, its long fingers reaching for my camera bag. As we made eye contact, it jumped down and swaggered away. I watched it stalking along, methodically testing all the other rooms to see if any doors were open. Bingo! The last room along from us had not only left the doors open, they had draped clothes all over the deck to dry. The animal snatched and sniffed the clothes and tossed them over the wall. I shouted, but we were far too far away to do anything – it was quite a long uphill hike from our room. Presumably there was nobody there otherwise they'd have been dealing with the situation, so even if we went there we wouldn't be able to get in. The adventurous baboon was joined by a companion and they disappeared into the interior. Heaven knows what they were getting up to. (We found out later – the room was totally trashed.)

Lunch was the usual luscious buffet of salads, roasts, curries, stir fries cooked to order, baked fish, vegetarian dishes, cheeses, flamboyant desserts and fresh fruit. Terry reached the fish just as the last portion was taken, and immediately the chef stepped forward to say he would prepare some more, which he did and delivered to the table. I know, it was hard eating all this food, but somebody had to do it. From the dining room we had an unhindered view down onto the plains. While we were lunching a couple of bulbul birds – similar to sparrows in size and colour, but with a bright yellow vent – came to peck up crumbs from vacated tables around us. A few yards away, a red-breasted sunbird posed obligingly, its multi-coloured iridescent feathers glistening metallically in the sun.

Apart from our infamous Scrabble match, Vivien and I hadn't had an opportunity to just sit and chat. Every minute of every day she had been watching over her guests, anticipating any needs or desires and making certain that our guides were well fed and looked after. After lunch, we went down to the swimming pool on a terrace below the main building and sat in the shade, wandering down memory lane, discussing 'the old days,' the people we knew, what had become of them and where they were now, the scandals, the paths that our lives have taken, and reminiscing about life in Kenya, and how lucky we were to have been so privileged – and where on earth had 55 years gone? It was as if the years had rolled back and we were once again just a pair of pony mad teenagers with our lives ahead of us.

'Do you want to play Scrabble?' Vivien asked.

'No,' I replied quickly. 'Let's just sit here and do nothing for an hour, shall we?'

All around us, varieties of birds hopped and chattered in the trees and the towering euphorbias, and scratched amongst the plants in the flower beds. Bright button eyes of rock hyrax peered out from the stone wall along the edge of the pool. They are the cutest little creatures, fat and floppy, dangling over rocks, curiously boneless, like beanbags. One had rolled over on its back on a rock, with its head hanging down. It looked like a soft toy carelessly tossed away. Another had ventured away from the wall and draped itself on the back of a sun lounger. We tried in vain to tempt them with morsels of bread, which the birds were quick to snatch up.

'Do you think I have shrunk?' Vivien asked.

She's tiny, not a gram of spare flesh, with the figure of a young girl. And yes, she seemed smaller than I remembered. We stood beside each other, and where once we were eye to eye, we are now eye to hairline.

'Yes, you are definitely shorter,' I said.

'I thought so. I wonder why?'

We are almost the same age, separated only by a few months. But where I have long been fairly sedentary, she is never still for a moment. She's impulsive, trusting, naïve beyond words, and a perfectionist. I was about to say that she reminded me of a pencil whittled down by constant sharpening, but the moment was lost when somebody called out: 'There's a warthog on the path,' so we went to investigate.

With their knobbly faces and curved tusks they have a rather fearsome appearance, but they are inoffensive, peaceful animals. Our visitor was standing contentedly grazing in a flowerbed. He trotted behind us along the path, down the steps and onto the paving surrounding the pool, where he snuffled a sun lounger as if considering lying down, peered into the water and contemplated his reflection for a while, before continuing on a leisurely perambulation around the perimeter. He stopped and examined a sign saying 'No diving' with apparent interest, and then, as if rather disappointed, ambled off down another pathway.

On our drive later that afternoon, I mentioned the hyrax to Dedan. I remembered being told long ago that the rock hyrax is the nearest living relative to the elephant, but having had the opportunity to examine both at close quarters the similarity had escaped me. Dedan, of course, had the answer. They are linked by their teeth – in most tusked animals the tusks are elongated canine teeth, but both the hyrax and the elephant's tusks develop from their incisors. Not that a hyrax's tusks are much to shout about. They're tiny. They also share with elephants the fact that their testicles are kept indoors, and their feet, which look as if they ought to end in claws, are spongy pads with neat rounded toenails. Only smaller, of course. Hyrax are herbivirous, and spend the daylight hours eating and sleeping. Either I have been one in a past life, or I'm going to try to come back as one in the next, because I know their lifestyle would suit me perfectly.

Before us was a great golden carpet flecked with moving grey dots as the herds grazed their way towards the river. It was an astonishing, almost surreal sight. The word Mara comes from the Maa meaning 'spotted,' referring to the trees and animals that give the landscape its flecked appearance. There were zebra and topi among them, but the vast bulk was a sea of murmuring wildebeeste. They formed small groups, clusters that broke apart and merged with others like a flock of birds, and sometimes lines of two abreast, heads nodding as they plodded purposefully following pathways worn in the grass, swirling around in all directions as if they didn't know whether they were coming or going. I often feel like that. Some stopped at the edge of the road to watch us with their long wise faces, and leapt in front of us at the last minute, inches from the vehicles, kicking their legs up behind them and chasing each other. Clowns.

The one big game animal that continued to elude us was the black rhino, and our guides were doing everything possible to find them. The vehicles went off in different directions, and as we drove around Dedan pointed out the myriad varieties of birds. He expected you to listen when he told you something. He wasn't talking to hear the sound of his voice, he wanted to share his knowledge and add to ours. 'What is that bird over there?', somebody asked, pointing. 'I told you that yesterday,' he responded. 'It's a stilt.'

While the rhino continued to be elusive, we were kept busy ticking off the birds in our little green books. Black chested harrier eagle – tick. Grassland pipits – tick. Yellow fronted canaries, red necked spur fowl, rufous necked larks. The ingenious yellow throated long claw, whose neck looks like a snake to deter predators when the bird is sitting on eggs, Nubian vultures and lappett-faced vultures, fork-tailed drongos and the spiteful little fiscal shrikes, white-browed coucals, wattled plovers, sooty chats, ox-peckers and egrets riding on a herd of buffalo, European white storks, bateleur eagles, and marabou nesting in the trees, just a few of the species living in the area. Tick, tick, tick.

Dedan mentioned casually that some birds are nidicolous and some are nidifugous. I surrendered and admitted I had no idea what those words meant.

He explained that the chicks of nidicolous birds are helpless and remain in the nest for some time after hatching, dependent upon their parents, while nidifugous chicks are ready to fend for themselves within a short time of hatching. You couldn't travel far with Dedan without learning new facts and words.

Then he added, of course you know that birds are either passerine or non-passerine? I didn't rise to the bait this time, just nodded wisely and Googled it later that evening. In case you don't know either, passerine birds have three toes in front that curl backwards, and one toe at the back curling forwards, enabling them to perch. Non-passerine birds have two front and two back toes and are generally birds that walk on the ground. These somewhat obscure facts are just the kind of thing that could come up in crosswords or quizzes, so they're worth remembering. Ostriches are neither passerine nor non-passerine, because they only have three toes.

We almost saw another leopard. It had been spotted behind some rocks, and we sat and waited for it to appear. When it did so it outwitted us all, as it dashed out in the opposite direction to where we were looking, and all we saw was a blur of spots and a very long tail. A little later, we noticed an antelope carcass high up in the fork of a tree, which is where leopards take their kills to protect them from other predators, so that they can eat undisturbed at their leisure.

It wasn't until the sun began to sink that we finally had to abandon the search for the black rhino and accept that it was one animal we were not destined to see. However, while there was still a glimmer of light, Dedan still had something up his sleeve. He pulled up beside a small puddle. *Gyrinus substriatus* he said, pointing at small black things darting about on the water.

'Common name is whirligigs. Very useful beetles that eat mosquito larvae.'

We watched the whirligigs dancing on the surface for a while, and it occurred to me that although people shudder at the thought of being out in the wild surrounded by creepy crawlies and snakes, not only hadn't we seen a single snake, neither had we noticed any insects at all apart from the *siafu* that got into Vivien's underwear at MKSC, and the solitary mosquito that I had despatched at Nakuru.

I would have very much liked to see some chameleons, but when I mentioned this none of the guides seemed enthusiastic about finding them. I used to find three-horned chameleons in the trees in my garden, and would put them on different coloured backgrounds to watch their skin change colour until they blended in perfectly. They are harmless and fascinating creatures, with their little clutchy feet and eyes that swivel independently of each other. When my cook, Mwiba, saw me holding them he was very anxious, and begged me not to touch them, because he believed they would make me ill, giving me tuberculosis. There wasn't any way I could change his mind. They are still associated with witchcraft and evil spirits, and I suppose it will take time to overcome the superstitions surrounding them, even among the most sophisticated and educated Kenyans.

Chapter Twenty-six

SPEAK SWAHILI: TAFADHALI – PLEASE

Our time in the wildlife reserves was over, and we were heading back to Nairobi. Although the recent rainfall had been relatively light, it had been sufficient to transform the dry, cracked soil into a quagmire of sticky black mud. The roads were impassable in places, gouged with deep tyre tracks, and vehicles had to be forced to divert onto the flatter parts, where puddles were hidden by lush green grass that had shot up overnight. It was a chance for the guides to play, racing each other over the slippery, skiddy terrain and spraying streams of mud into the air. Vivien laughed, pointing to Kamara as his vehicle fishtailed around. 'That is what he loves,' she smiled.

Dedan joined in the impromptu race, but I sensed a lack of commitment.

'Do you enjoy this?' I asked.

'No,' he replied frankly. 'Very dirty, and can damage the vehicle.'

We passed a large tanker carrying liquid petroleum gas – emblazoned with 'Danger' painted in large red letters. The thing was tipped right over on its side and partially sunken into the mud. Several motorcyclists, a couple of men and a few cattle were standing around studying the situation from different angles. Knowing the ingenuity of Kenyans, and their long experience with dealing with impassable roads and impossible tasks, I was confident the tanker would be upright and on its way before too long.

As we passed Kichwa Tembo (Elephant's Head) camp, Dedan remarked that it was there he took the first step to becoming a safari guide, and like David, it was largely by accident. At the time he was a very good football player, and his brother, who worked as a chef at the camp, recruited him to join their football team. Seeing what a valuable addition he was to the team, the camp gave him a job starting as a room steward. Jonathan Scott, zoologist and wildlife photographer and presenter of Big Cat Diary on BBC television, and ornithologist Brian Finch (what a great name for an ornithologist!) ran training sessions for the camp guides, and Dedan began finishing his work early so that he could attend. He then continued his training by going on game drives to increase his knowledge. He was promoted to the position of naturalist and standby guide until he eventually qualified to become a fully licensed guide.

Once out of the mud and onto the tarmac, we promptly had a puncture – the second that Dedan's Land Cruiser had suffered on our trip. If having a puncture could be regarded as lucky, then at least it wasn't in the sticky black mud. A group of children gathered to watch impassively while Steve, who seemed to enjoy anything that involved messing about with vehicles, changed the wheel and Dedan managed to remain immaculate as ever.

In 2002, President Mwai Kibaki introduced free and compulsory primary school education for every child in Kenya. From what I was told, it didn't work that well in practice because the teachers employed by the State were very poorly paid, consequently there weren't enough and so classes were overcrowded, and those parents who were able to afford it preferred to send their children to private schools. A few days ago we had heard that the State teachers were on strike because they had fought for an improved salary through the courts and won their case, but still they had not received any increase.

When we began passing groups of small children walking beside the road, wearing school satchels on their backs, I asked if the teachers had now returned to work. Dedan replied that the strike was still on, but the children took themselves to school and taught themselves, such is their passion for education and their understanding of its importance.

There was something very poignant about these children – they were only little – smart in their uniforms even if their feet were bare, marching briskly along the dusty roadsides to try to teach themselves.

Driving through Narok, my thoughts returned to that little girl who was hit by the car. I don't think I'll ever get the image of her lying in the road out of my mind.

The Mara Serena had provided picnic boxes for our lunch, and we stopped for an hour at a rest point/loo/curio shop. As usual we were quickly engaged by enthusiastic salesmen, and as usual there were no prices marked, and as usual when you asked the price of an article it was met with the standard response that the more articles you bought, the cheaper it would work out, and as usual before you could think, you found a basket draped over your arm. The shop was the size of an aircraft hangar, crammed with superb wood and soapstone carvings of every animal and in sizes ranging from minute to almost life-sized, jewellery of semi-precious stones, beads, shells and metals, paintings, animal skin shields, *rungus*, ashtrays and *shukas*. The moment you stopped to look at something, you found it pressed into the basket. I would have loved one of the beaded belts like the one David wore, not only because it was beautiful, but it would keep my trousers from falling down every time I stood up, and release one of my hands. Alas, it was more than we could afford. Our funds were limited and there were still a few days left that would involve tips and other expenses, but I did cave in and end up with another necklace to swell my collection to five. When the salesman became too insistent, I told him: 'We are not American – we are British' and I saw the realisation in his eyes that we were a lost cause.

Entrepreneurs had set up business all along the roadside. A motor repair 'workshop' that was just a sign and a shack. The car wash that comprised a bucket and some cloths. Restaurants, hotels, beauty salons, charcoal sellers, churches, livestock, handfuls of vegetables, second-hand clothing and gleaming pimped *boda bodas*. Every business carried a grandiose title: Jubilee, Excelsior, Best, Greatest, Supreme, Starbucks, Paradise Hotel, Hard Rock Café... A plot of land bore a notice painted in large letters: Buyers beware – this plot is not for sale.

The drive back to Nairobi led across the escarpment, giving a dazzling panorama of the Rift Valley below. The road was heavily congested and sometimes slightly hair-raising. Streams of overladen heavy goods vehicles came from the opposite direction at breakneck speed around bends on the edge of a long sheer drop. The maintenance of the vehicles was suspect, and brake reliability potentially non-existent, so it was largely a case of luck whether the vehicles successfully negotiated this road. Not all did. Seconds before we passed, a car had hurtled off the road and bounced hundreds of feet down the side of the escarpment. People had stopped their vehicles and rushed to peer over the edge. We learned on the radio a while later that the driver had miraculously survived and was on his way to hospital. I could only imagine that he must have grown wings.

I remembered a crazy drive on this road when I was eighteen and had been invited to spend the weekend with my friend who lived at what was then Thomson's Falls. Two Kenya cowboys as they were known – English settlers notorious for their wild ways – were on their way there for a polo match, and offered me a lift in their open-top sports car. I was sitting in the back when the driver, who was going at a goodly pace, suddenly stretched both arms in the air, yawned loudly and announced that he was tired and going to get in the back for a rest. Without slowing the pace, he climbed over his seat and sank down beside me, closing his eyes, while I sat frozen like a rabbit in headlights while the car drove itself. I remember squeaking as the other passenger, equally casually, moved across into the driving seat and took over. Those kinds of things happened; the young men I knew at the time all drove too fast (one killed himself), played rugby and didn't think it had been much of a game unless they broke something, rode horses too fast, jumped jumps too high, drank too much. In short, they lived life to the full, and in those days they could get away with it. Life was so carefree, health and safety were just words. Seat belts? What seat belts? Surprisingly, most of us survived.

The intoxicating aroma of roasted mealies – corn cobs – wafted in from roadside stalls. It reminded me of a visit to one of the *banlieues* in Paris that has a predominantly immigrant population. There's a vibrant exciting market on Sunday mornings, where one enterprising trader pushes around a supermarket trolley filled with charcoal on which he roasts corn cobs.

On the other side of the road overlooking the plunge down to the Rift Valley, there were curio shops selling sheepskin and goat skins, beadware and curios, and a public convenience, all built out of planks of wood, spindly branches and sheets of corrugated iron, and balanced on the very edge of the precipice. One of them actually had an upper floor.

Then we were in the lush green tea-growing highlands of Limuru where as a teenager I used to follow the Limuru Drag Hunt on Sundays. Again those bitter-sweet memories flooded back. The grooms hacked the horses over on the Saturday, and stayed on whichever farm was hosting the hunt. When I arrived on Sunday morning, Cinderella would be gleaming, her mane perfectly plaited and her leather saddlery soft and fragrant. Those were such happy occasions, the hunt servants in their colourful livery, hounds barking (or speaking if you wish to be correct) with excitement, glasses of sherry to steady the nerves, the horses whinnying their excitement as the field moved off after the scent that had been laid down by a runner. We didn't hunt animals, but chased a sack of meat dragged along the ground by a rider earlier in the morning. It was thrilling, exhilarating, frequently frightening. Cinderella was headstrong and excitable, hard to hold back when we galloped, and more than once we overtook everybody including the Master (a cardinal sin) but in this sociable group nobody stood on ceremony too much. Once the hunt had finished and we were back at the farm, the grooms took the horses to cool off and rest before the journey home, while we ate from tables laden with curries. Watching the green fields as we passed, I found myself both smiling at the memory of those days and holding back tears, incredulous to think that it was more than 50 years ago.

That night we spent back at the lovely Nairobi Serena. I have a hate relationship with smart phones. Probably I'm the only person in the world who finds them more trouble than they are worth. I don't know why because I consider myself quite savvy with technical matters. Unless it's a hardware fault, I can generally sort out a computer that is misbehaving (although of course I did need Jessica to solve the upside down screen). At home, I am the one who sets up the television, the satellite, the recorder and any other peripherals, and I'm even fairly au fait with the intricate Olympus menu system on our cameras. But I simply don't have the patience with the smart phone and I don't understand the obsession with having the latest model and the way people seem to be permanently glued to them, even when dining out or staying with friends. I find them intrusive and anti-social and altogether very irritating. Mine seems to know how I feel about it, and it's a given that on the rare occasions when I may need to use it, either the battery will be flat or it won't be able to pick up a signal. Still, I'd taken the thing with me to keep a check on my email, and for the alarm function. With us having had to be up at horrible o'clocks we had needed something to wake us, and for that it had performed satisfactorily. Before dinner, we packed our luggage in preparation for our departure next morning, and I left the phone on the writing desk.

It woke us the following morning as requested, and we put our bags outside the door to be taken down, but when we returned from breakfast the phone was no longer on the desk. It wasn't anywhere to be found. We searched the drawers, my backpack, anywhere I could have mistakenly put it, but it had vanished. I was not particularly concerned, it was a cheap thing and I didn't need it any more – no more early morning calls – but I mentioned it casually to Vivien. Oh dear, what a mistake that was. Ignoring my protests, she put the hotel on full-scale security alert. Our room was searched, every nook and cranny, even under the mattress, and there was no sign of the wretched thing. They telephoned the person who had cleaned and made up the room, who had finished their shift and gone home, and told them to come back in. I was totally mortified and pleaded for the matter to be dropped, but the wheels were in motion and couldn't be stopped. The hotel manager asked if I would let them put my bags through the scanner and there it was, tucked away inside my suitcase. My humiliation was complete and the head of security was stone-faced in response to my apology. I've thought of that incident several times since, and I think what had happened was that whoever collected our luggage saw the phone on the desk and had put it into the case. We had frequently left our cameras, watches and the computer unattended and had never been given any reason to doubt the honesty of the staff wherever we had stayed.

Our guides joined us for breakfast and despite Vivien's

encouragement and assurances, they unanimously didn't like grapefruit. :)

Chapter Twenty-seven

SPEAK SWAHILI: MINGI – MANY

One of the friends I had left behind in Kenya all those years ago was a beautiful, funny, charismatic girl. Her name was Valerie and she was David Sheldrick's daughter. We had kept in touch for a few years when I left Kenya, and met up on her occasional visits to England. There was always a slight mystery surrounding those visits, but she never explained them and I never asked. Her letters stopped and mine went unanswered until one was returned unopened. This happened long before the arrival of the internet, and I was unable to find out what had become of her.

Years later, when I first heard about the David Sheldrick Elephant Orphanage, I wrote to Dame Daphne Sheldrick to ask for news of Valerie, and learned that she had died very young from a long-standing condition that she knew about but had never mentioned. Her visits to England had been to see specialists who unfortunately had been unable to save her. I was thinking of her as we drove to Langata.

We had already been pretty close to elephants, but this morning we were going to get even closer when we visited the orphanage on the outskirts of Nairobi, where we would be able to mingle with and touch the little elephants. We left the hotel early to avoid the worst of Nairobi's traffic jams. I could not recognise anything of the Langata where I once kept Cinderella stabled on a farm overlooked by the Ngong Hills. Like Nairobi, it had changed beyond recognition. The elephant orphanage hadn't even existed when I left. Dame Daphne Sheldrick set it up in 1977 to continue the work of her husband David, one of Kenya's best-known and most loved pioneers of national parks and the rescuing and raising wildlife victims of poaching and accident. The majority of their orphans are elephants, but no wild animal in need is overlooked, and they have saved giraffe, rhino, antelope and even baby ostriches.

As we stood excitedly in the car park waiting for the gate to open, I think our guides were looking forward to this visit just as much as we were even though they have all visited the orphanage dozens if not hundreds of times.

Edwin Lusichi is the head keeper at the orphanage and had been working at the Trust for 16 years. He has the air of somebody who is completely happy with his job and life. Before he took us to meet the residents, he talked about the work and aims of the orphanage.

The Trust operates aerial surveillance over the parks and reserves to spot poachers and wounded animals, while ground patrols search for snares, and the recent introduction of dog patrols has been highly effective in hunting the poachers. It is not only poaching that threatens elephants, but also the human conflict and accidents caused by falling down wells or becoming trapped in mud. The Trust has elicited the support of local communities to keep a watch and advise them when an animal needs help, so the flying veterinary service can be mobilised to reach the victim quickly, tranquillising and treating, or if necessary, humanely euthanising it.

Sometimes baby elephants become unavoidably separated from their herd, and if every effort to reunite them fails the only course of action is to bring them to the Trust's orphanage. Once safely captured, they are flown in one of the Trust's aircraft to Nairobi. During the flight, they will already be receiving treatment to calm and hydrate them. When the plane lands in Nairobi, an awaiting vehicle drives them to the stockade of the Trust, and into the hands of the devoted, passionate keepers there who will nurture them and act as surrogate mothers. This is a 24-hour, 7-day week responsibility for the first eighteen months of the baby elephant's life. Their keeper will be with them at all times, sleeping beside them in their stalls in the stockade, accompanying them on their daily walks out into the park, always on hand to protect, reassure and comfort them, just as their mothers would do in the wild. They are easily frightened by unfamiliar things – a snake or hailstorm may panic them and cause them to run away and get lost, and they depend on their keepers to find them and take them back to safety. Red *shukas* were traditionally worn by Maasai warriors, the age-old enemy of lions, and the keepers wear these to warn the lions away when they take the little elephants into the park.

Despite their great size, elephants are the most emotionally sensitive of all animals, and suffer extreme stress. Losing their mothers breaks their hearts, so these babies, who are totally dependent, are fragile and have to be treated with the utmost tenderness. Saving a baby elephant is a long-term commitment, as each of them will require dedicated care and support for years before they are able and ready to become independent. It is an undertaking of monumental devotion.

They cannot all be saved. Some are too weak or have sustained injuries that are too severe. They may have ingested foul water into their lungs, or been infested by parasites. But the learning process continues in finding ways to treat them. Dame Daphne Sheldrick is the first person to have perfected the milk formula for baby elephants and rhinos, but their survival depends on much more than food. Without the support of their herd, they have to learn to live as elephants, to recover from the stress of losing their families, and learn to love life so that they can eventually return to the wild.

Since its inception, the Trust has successfully raised and

returned 160 elephants to the wild where they have integrated into wild herds and raised their own young. These wild units are under constant surveillance, and the orphans return to greet their keepers and show that they have not forgotten those who became their surrogate parents. At the end of 2014, one of the females rehabilitated into a wild herd came to the stockades to give birth to her second baby, surrounded by members of her herd and in the company of the keepers who had cared for her during her dependent years. The old saying that an elephant never forgets isn't just a saying, it is a fact. They will remember all their lives those humans who have helped them. Recently a bull with a poisoned dart embedded in it had made its way to one of the Trust's locations knowing that there it would find the help and life-saving treatment it needed.

The saving and successful rearing of the baby elephants is only one part of the Trust's work. Their long term goal is to create safe havens in the wild, and they work with the Kenyan Wildlife Service and Kenya Forest Service as well as local communities towards this end. Education of the people is key to underpinning the safety of the wildlife, and the Trust organises school visits to the orphanage, funds field visits to Tsavo so the children can see the elephants in the wild, and donates equipment to schools in the Tsavo area as well as offering free medical treatment to communities there, including eye and dental care. In drought-stricken areas, the Trust has established boreholes, as well as erecting and maintaining both electrical and bee-hive fencing to control the conflict between humans encroaching into what was once wildlife habitat and the animals that try to reclaim that habitat.

Before leading us to where the babies would come for their morning feed, Edwin had some words of advice for our safety. We should not shout, as it could startle the babies, and he warned us not to get between them and their bottles, and not to squat down and risk being bowled over.

He led us to the feeding area where jumbo-sized (excuse me, I couldn't resist that) bottles of milk were lined up then we watched as the keepers walked up a slight slope and disappeared behind a clump of bushes. We waited silently for the orphans to arrive – I found myself holding my breath with excitement. When they came, trotting behind their keepers, I don't think there was a single heart between us that didn't melt at the sight of these enchanting babies hurrying towards their bottles. They were bright paprika red from the dust, with *shukas* tied to their backs to protect them from the sun.

Baby's breakfast, David Sheldrick Wildlife Trust Elephant Orphanage

I did say many chapters ago that I would disgrace myself before our visit was over, and this is where it happened. Forgetting Edwin's advice, I'm ashamed to admit that I inadvertently squealed with excitement and wanting to get a video of the infants, I got between them and their waiting milk. Suddenly, there was a lot of loud, excited yelling and I found myself flying through the air as Dedan grabbed me and swung me out of the path of several tons of elephants bearing down on their breakfast. Before our safari, Vivien had said that it would be the guides who would make or break our trip, and indeed they had. Not only do I owe Dedan my thanks for educating me, increasing my vocabulary and for constantly reminding me to do up my shoelaces, I quite possibly owe him my life. I am quite proud of the fact that during this incident I managed to hold on to my camera and keep filming.The orphans stood there guzzling their milk. The very tiny ones needed help from the keepers, while the larger ones wrapped their trunks expertly around the bottles and held them by themselves, gulping and dribbling milk in their excitement.

Did you know that young baby elephants are adorably hairy, with thick fringes of woolly hair on their ears, whiskery lips and little tufts on their heads and bodies? Like giant soft toys. After they had satiated themselves, they played with each other just like puppies, wrestling and rolling, splashing in a muddy pool, playing with a hose pipe, and intertwining their little trunks. We were able to walk among and stroke them, which they seemed to enjoy. One of them wound its trunk around Terry's arm, holding it gently and guiding it into its mouth.

All of us have supported the orphanage by adopting a baby elephant. The minimum annual fee is only the cost of a modest meal out for two people, so little to contribute to the incredible and vital work that these people are doing to save Kenya's elephants.

Terry's adopted baby is a little girl called Mbegu. She had a traumatic experience when the Kenyan Wildlife Services had been forced to shoot her mother who had killed a villager. The herd had stampeded, leaving behind the 7-

week-old orphan. Not satisfied with the death of her mother, the angry villagers wanted to kill the baby too, and they had imprisoned and tortured her. The Trust had had to engage in lengthy, delicate diplomacy before the villagers reluctantly agreed to release her so that she could be brought to the orphanage. Despite her frightening start to life, Mbegu had flourished and at just over a year old was already showing maternal instincts to other orphans.

My adopted baby was Simotua, an orphan rescued a year ago, and now two years old. He was a victim of poaching, found with a terrible spear wound that had penetrated his trunk right through to his skull, and an equally dreadful wound to his leg where he had been caught in a snare. He seemed to be doing well despite the gaping hole in his trunk where you could see and hear his breathing. We were all horrified by this dreadful injury. David and Dedan were particularly moved. 'How could anybody do this?' they asked. I tried to approach him but he was a little shy and despite the size and the fact that he was considerably bigger and stronger than I was, I was very conscious of not doing anything to frighten him. I held out a branch of green leaves which he accepted gently, before turning away and following the rest of the herd back into the trees. Sadly, little Simotua would only survive for a few more months after our visit despite all the care he was given.

The smallest babies barely came up to my waist, while the larger orphans were as tall as the keepers. My admiration for the keepers is beyond words. Elephant infants weigh about 200 pounds at birth and can gain 2 to 3 pounds a day, so by my calculation at one year old they could weigh the best part of 1,000 pounds, or half a ton. They have an extremely close bond with their 'mother' keepers, who are with them constantly until they are ready to be reintegrated into the wild, but they are nevertheless still wild animals, and VERY BIG INDEED, immensely strong, and can be boisterous and awkward at times. It was so touching to watch the relationship between them, trunks reaching up to nuzzle faces, curling around arms, tapping at clothing, following their keepers, and the men as tender and gentle with them as any human mother with her child.

A couple of ostriches called Pea and Pod, found as abandoned chicks, had become an integral part of the nursery, acting as cuddly toys for the elephants. Edwin took us on a tour of the nursery to see the orphans' sleeping quarters with deep hay for bedding and raised platforms where their keepers spend the night.

In a large stockade fenced with sturdy poles, we finally came face to face with that difficult-to-find animal, the black rhino. Even after walking among the elephants, we were taken aback by the enormity of this creature which weighs 3,000 pounds and is the size of a caravan. Although considerably smaller than a white rhino, this fellow is still gigantic.

Edwin described how Maxwell had been found wandering as a baby, blind and rejected by his mother. When it became obvious that the baby rhino could not and would not be able to survive in the wild, and his mother refused to accept him, he was taken to the orphanage. Several operations to repair his eyesight were unsuccessful, and so he had been living there for ten years, in a spacious stockade with plenty of room to explore. Ten years is a long time to be alone, I remarked to Edwin. Didn't Maxwell ever get lonely?

Edwin replied that black rhino are solitary creatures by nature, and Maxwell is very content and safe from poachers who would kill him for his fine horns. There is a female rhino, once an orphan at the Trust herself but now returned to the wild, who visits Maxwell from time to time. Despite his fearsome size and appearance, and the reputation of the rhino for being aggressive, he is apparently a docile fellow –

when he had found his way out of the stockade a couple of years previously, he had been coaxed back in with a bottle of milk and some bananas.

Our visit was over too soon. I think, given the opportunity we would all have happily spent the whole day there. If anybody had told us that one day we would be walking around in a herd of elephants, we'd have thought they had taken leave of their senses. Terry said it was the most magical memory of his visit to Kenya. He often talks about it even now.

Chapter Twenty-eight

SPEAK SWAHILI: TEACHER – MWALIMU

As we left Langata, I overheard Vivien talking to Kamara in Swahili, debating whether we ought to have a police escort to our next destination. After some discussion they decided it would be safe for us to go on our own.

Colonisation introduced sophisticated medicine, education and an overall improvement in the standard of living for many in Kenya. Consequently, fertility increased, infant mortality decreased and people recovered from illnesses that would once have been fatal. Malaria has been almost eradicated in Nairobi. This has resulted in the population exploding from 6 million in 1950 to over 48 million in 2017, and therein lies the problem – there is not enough work for everyone, there is not enough housing and that is why an estimated 2.5 million people (60% of Nairobi's population) – live in slums like Mathare and Kibera, the largest slum in Kenya, in fact one of the largest in the world and home to a quarter of a million people.

When Kenya regained independence from Britain in 1963, the new government rewarded those supporters who had fought for that independence by giving them land in the suburbs of Nairobi. One such place was an area of about 1.5 square miles a little way from Nairobi city centre, close to the upmarket residential suburbs of Lavington and Karen. The area is called Ngando.

The problem was that the new landowners did not have the means to build decent housing, so a town of tin shacks grew up. A water supply was installed, but the residents did not have the means to pay their water bills, and so they were disconnected. The landowners effectively had land that was of very little use to them. When the building boom began, workers were flocking to Nairobi and they needed cheap accommodation. Ngando's landowners now had a source of income. However, little was done to improve the buildings, and the worst problem was one of hygiene – there were very few lavatories, forcing people to relieve themselves outside wherever they could, and no facilities for waste disposal. The only available water supply was from shallow boreholes. Borehole water is high in fluoride which can have a detrimental effect on the teeth of children, staining them permanently brown.

As men brought their families to live with them and younger men married and raised their own children, the population of Ngando grew and the landowners built more and more tinny cheap and insanitary houses. Today some 40,000 people live in the slum of Ngando, prisoners of their own poverty, working in the lowest paid sector as labourers, gardeners, messengers, house maids or cleaners, or creating small businesses as hairdressers, tailors, butchers and shopkeepers.

Even for hard-working slum dwellers, life in Nairobi is expensive. They have to travel to work, feed and clothe themselves and their families, and of course pay their rent. Many families will frequently have only one meal a day. Those who are unemployed go off in the early morning to seek work, forced to leave their children to fend for themselves. Primary education is free, but there are the associated costs of uniforms and materials. Sometimes schools will allow the parents time to find the school fees, but often when the debt burden grows too heavy, the family will simply move their children to another school.

Once children have finished their primary education, many families cannot afford to continue paying school fees, and their children will have to find their own ways to survive

– by thieving, prostitution or drug dealing, and how then will they ever escape to find a decent and secure future? Life is hard in the slum. It's overcrowded, unhygienic and dangerous.

That was our destination.

Vivien is well-known in Ngando, and she was confident that we would be safe there. On the way, down roads that I remembered as wide open spaces, we passed rustic shopping arcades where small businesses displayed their goods beside the road. Soft furnishings, an upholstered three-piece suite; intricately carved wooden bed heads, gaily painted wrought iron four-posters; a car wash/carpet cleaner; beaten metal ornamental animals. Everywhere there was evidence of the ingenuity, vision and hard work of people determined to better themselves.

Entering Ngando was a fairly unnerving experience, driving through narrow muddy alleys lined with shacks, shanties, heaps of waste, puddles of sewage and broken-up road. Thin dogs and goats scrabbled amongst the rubbish. Some people watched silently as our convoy drove through. Some stared impassively, a few raised a hand in greeting. The small children all smiled with the instant smile of Kenyan children, shyly, waving. It smelled really bad there. Everything looked filthy, even the humble shops, butchers, mobile phone charging stations, tailors, all tumbling down, with pieces of sacking and plastic sheeting tied to bits of wood with string. I'd been photographing all through our journey – albeit surreptitiously on occasion, but it felt insensitive to photograph these people and the conditions in which they were living. The houses were little more than cells, with mud or sheet iron walls and roofs, dirt floors, no windows, no electricity, no water, no lavatories. But it was after all their home, and photographing it somehow seemed wrong, underlining just how squalid it was. We all put our cameras away.

We were going to visit the Hope Streams Academy, a school that aims to reduce the number of children who will end up on the streets, and to offer a decent education and the chance of a better future to the young of this miserable place – miserable in the sense of appearance rather than attitude, because most of the people seemed quite bright and cheerful as they went about their business. Music mingled with the smell of roasting meat. What the population lack in wealth, they more than make up for in resilience.

At the end of a pot-holed track, we came to a rough gate where a tall, fierce-looking guard waved us into a parking area beside a couple of sunbathing dogs and a few wooden cages housing chickens. Below, in a small valley, stood the collection of buildings that are the Hope Streams Academy. The school principal, Patrick Madunda, a large jovial man, came forward to shake our hands, followed by the school's teachers, dressed in their ill-fitting best. I was so moved by the dignity of these people who live and work in these dreadful conditions that I could feel tears rolling down my face. They each wore a paper label giving their name and their function. Florence, Class 3 teacher. Norah, the school cook. Simon, Class 4 teacher. Mildred, the smiling secretary.

The children had decorated their faces with chalk in abstract designs. Some wore the Academy's purple and white uniform, while others were dressed in dirty torn clothes, and others in a combination of both; some were barefoot, others wore shoes that were far too big for them. One small girl was wearing a pair of men's black lace-up shoes that were many sizes too large. She could have comfortably fitted both feet into one shoe, and I have no idea how she managed to walk in them.

As we walked down the hill towards their classrooms, they were chanting: 'Visitors, we love you. Visitors we love you.' Some were waving posters: 'Thank you Vivien, we love you more.' 'Thank you Jessica and the church group.'

'Welcome visitors and feel at home.' The tinies were smiling and giggling, excited by the activity; some of the older children looked as if they were enjoying themselves, others were curious, some bewildered and a few looked stressed and anxious. They understood that our visit would bring benefits to them, and they had been rehearsing their singing, reciting and dancing to entertain us.

School principal Patrick Madunda is himself a resident of the Ngando slum. He is justifiably proud of the school, and the high academic standards achieved by the under-privileged children. His job is not an easy one. From school fees collected and donations from supporters, Patrick has to pay the teachers and the taxes and buy materials. He also tries to provide meals for those children who will not be fed at home. Many of them will only have one meal a day, and it is difficult for a hungry child to concentrate on lessons.

There is not enough money to buy school books for each child, to pay for transport to take sick children to hospital, insufficient resources for extra-curricular activities, games, educational trips, student exchanges, insufficient funds to support those children who are at risk and in need of extra care. There is no money for paid holidays, sick pay, travel expenses, bonuses, loans, housing, maternity leave for the teachers, not enough to pay the teachers wages commensurate with their skill – they can earn more working as maids or messengers, thus there is a turnover of staff and difficulty in recruiting qualified teachers. There is too little money to pay for the entrance fee for the children to take the exams that are their passport to higher education. Many of the pupils at the academy are high achievers with the potential to eventually go to university to earn degrees, but they cannot do that without financial assistance.

Patrick juggles what little there is, prioritising in the best interests of the pupils, which means that frequently taxes have to go unpaid, which results in Patrick being arrested and held until somebody can bail him out.

As we listened to him talking, we realised just how every cent is important. He told us how he saved money by making the blackboards and whiteboards for the classrooms himself, buying the materials – chipboard and white formica for the whiteboards, and for the blackboards plywood and blackboard paint. But for each board, somebody must travel to Nairobi city to collect the material – transport is expensive. With more funds, the materials could be bought in bulk, saving those costly journeys.

With no electric lighting in the schoolrooms, the children struggle to read from blackboards. But where blackboards can use cheap chalk, readily available in the slums, the chalk dust can be a health hazard to the small children. Whiteboards are easier to read, but require the more expensive felt marker pens that quickly dry out. Teachers not used to using them may forget to replace the tops. Felt pens are only available in Nairobi city, which means a time-consuming and expensive journey using money that could be put to better use. Limited funds do not enable them to buy in bulk. Nothing is simple and the more you listen to Patrick, the more you realise the size of the task he faces.

Even with the modest fees paid by parents, aid from the Clinton Foundation to pay teachers' salaries and donations from well-wishers, there is never enough to cover all the expenses. What the school does have are two assets: firstly, they own the land upon which it stands, which is increasing in value as the city expands. And secondly Patrick himself, a man who is humble, honest, hard-working and irrevocably committed to doing everything within his power to ensure that the Ngando children have a future away from the slum.

When it was time for the children to perform their party pieces for us, the little tots recited poems and waved their hands – there was a certain amount of giggling and looking for reassurance, then the older children who were more confident and earnest.

A group of girls aged about twelve appeared. They started singing and dancing with tremendous enthusiasm and energy, and with that rhythm that is uniquely African. Their bodies moved sinuously and seemingly without effort, their behinds waggling with a life of their own, arms waving, shoulders shimmying, feet shuffling.

I was so fascinated watching them that I let down my guard, and before I had time to react, a smiling, nubile, hip-swaying girl shuffled over to me and took me by the hand, gently but with determination and led me to the front row of their dancing exhibition. And there I stood, swaying feebly, bra-less, bare-faced, hair akimbo, well aware that my trousers were inexorably sliding down over my hips – it wouldn't be long before they landed around my ankles and I would become the unwitting star of the show. I moved my hips gingerly from side to side at the same time as applying my elbows to the waistband of my trousers in an effort to keep them in place. As much as I told myself that nobody was looking at me, that this was the children's show, let's be honest, one white face amongst thirty coloured was bound to stand out. The children showed no signs of tiring. They were singing and dancing with a preternatural energy, and after what was probably no more than five minutes but felt like eternity, I was able to disentangle my hand and jiggle back to my seat.

After the children's performances, we toured the classrooms, bordered with little flowerbeds, constructed of corrugated iron sheets and brightly painted with fruit and kitchen utensils and scenes from *Winnie the Pooh*. The only light inside the classrooms came from transparent plastic bottles cut into the roof panels and filled with a mixture of water and bleach, which give off a surprisingly powerful light.

As part of their own fund-raising efforts the pupils make souvenirs, mostly beaded jewellery, and so we bought some more necklaces and matching bracelets. That brings my necklace count to six and the bracelets to seven. I had not previously noticed that my hands were unnaturally large, but they plainly are because not one of the bracelets would fit over them.

As You Like It Safaris have supported the school for many years, introducing clients and encouraging them to undertake fund-raising campaigns which have provided, among other things, the paving slabs for the floors of the classrooms so that the children and teachers are no longer walking in mud when it rains. Situated as it is in a valley, during the rainy season the place becomes a quagmire when the mud from the surrounding area is washed down the hill. Two giant tanks donated by a Nevada Rotary club capture rain and store rainwater, giving the school access to their own water.

The big moment arrived when the children's patience was rewarded and it was time to distribute the gifts that we had brought. Our guides and Paul, the retained taxi driver were here to help. They had laid out all the gifts of clothing, games, toys, educational aids and snacks on long trestles, and the children lined up in an orderly queue, taking their turn to approach. The infants went first, one little girl still in nappies, wearing a pair of woolly tights and a stretchy bodysuit that was too small to do up, with coloured ribbons in her wispy hair. It was truly humbling to see how thrilled they were to be given a banana, a packet of biscuits and a carton of juice. The older pupils received their gifts solemnly, and what struck me most powerfully was the way all these children all wore smiles, and were full of confidence and carried their heads high and shoulders back, no matter that they were barefoot or dressed in ragged clothes. They were so proud of themselves.

When all the presents had been distributed and it was time for us to leave, somebody took off their trainers and handed them to Florence, Class 3 teacher. Others followed suit until she was standing there beaming, cradling an armful of second-hand shoes like a precious gift, and most of our group were barefoot.

Chapter Twenty-nine

SPEAK SWAHILI: COFFEE – KAHAWA

When we had first told friends that we were going to Kenya I was taken aback by some of the remarks.

'Are you crazy?' they asked. 'Those people will slit your throat as soon as look at you.'

'My god, you must be nuts. Have you no idea how DANGEROUS it is there? They are all terrorists.'

'Wow, you're brave. All those diseases and poisonous snakes and insects. Not for me.'

This one was a classic: 'What on earth do you want to go there for? You can see all those animals in zoos.'

And so on.

All those who made comments like that had one thing in common, which was that they had never been to Kenya. Where on earth did people get these ideas from? That's a rhetorical question. Their views were based on what they had read or heard on the media. The Westgate bombing – which had happened within spitting distance of where our family had first lived when we came to Kenya – and Al Shabab attacks in the Northern Frontier Province had been widely publicised across the world. That coverage gave the impression that the entire country was in turmoil, with gunmen and bombers lurking on every corner mowing down tourists. Travel advisories warned visitors to avoid Kenya – it was a 'hot-bed of terrorism' according to an ill-advised and ill-informed comment on CNN when President Obama had visited the country earlier in the year.

In contrast, all my friends who had ever visited or lived in Kenya said how jealous they were, how they wished they could come too, how lucky we were, because they know the magic, the spectacular landscape, the glorious weather, the friendliness of the people and the wonders of the wildlife.

It's a strange thing that Kenya seems to have been so often singled out for criticism, as if no tourist was safe there, or there was no danger in any other part of the world. Kenyans are not terrorists. The majority are hard-working people trying to make a living and better their families, and the military are actively fighting against terrorism.

During the 1970s, 1980s and 1990s, bombings in London were a regular occurrence. I don't recall England being branded as a hotbed of terrorism. We went about our daily lives as normal. People were warned to be vigilant, not to boycott the country.

A couple of months before our trip, a teenager had walked into a church in Charleston in the United States and slaughtered nine people attending a service.

While we were in transit on our way to Kenya, a gunman had tried to hold up a train in France. The following day twelve people died when a plane crashed at an air show in southern England.

As a fatalist, I believe that our lives and deaths are embedded in us as certainly as our DNA. Call it kismet, karma, predestination, destiny, fate or divine will. I'm sure many people will disagree, but it's my personal belief. I believe that death will come for you when it's ready. Worrying about it isn't going to make any difference. If we become afraid to step out of our homes for fear of an accident or an attack, do we even dare stay in them? What if another plane falls from the sky right where we are sitting?

Nobody in their right mind would recommend visiting a war zone for a holiday, or roaming around in dangerous areas after dark. We have to be sensible but we can't let fear be our constant companion otherwise we'll never go anywhere or do anything. What is the difference between the dangers of the Western world where acts of terror are increasing, and the dangers of Kenya where they happen from time to time?

I was no more worried about our safety in Kenya than I would be driving my car down the lane near our home in France.

Chapter Thirty

SPEAK SWAHILI: CHAKULA – FOOD

Our journey was almost over, and my heart felt a little heavier by the hour. Some of our group would be leaving in the afternoon, and in two days time we'd be on our way home. I was going to savour every minute until then.

Muthaiga, our final destination, is Nairobi's most swanky suburb. It's always been the chosen location for embassies and the ultra-wealthy, an area of imposing properties in landscaped grounds of sprinklered lawns behind tall walls and ornate gates. If you want to impress, this is the place to live.

Given my newly-found feelings about Kenya's colonial past and the woeful poverty of the slum we had just visited, I suppose it's hypocritical of me, but I have to confess that I absolutely loved floating back in time to the days when Britannia ruled the waves and Kenya was a colony, as we arrived at Muthaiga Country Club. It is still very much the gentlemen's club that it was designed to be over a hundred years ago, the place where those pioneering British aristocrats came to stay when they could get away from the rough life on their farms, where they could have a decent bath and mix with their own kind, which did not include civil servants or tradesmen who were not welcome. Money can't buy you admittance here. Unless you are a member or the guest of a member, you won't be coming in. To become a member, you must be proposed by an existing member and seconded by another. After all three have filled in and submitted the relevant forms, the applicant must wait patiently to be invited to meet with the committee members, and then must continue to wait patiently, possibly for many months, to learn whether their application has been successful.

Only two years previously women – or ladies – were allowed to become members in their own right. Fortunately we all knew how to behave, as members are responsible for the behaviour of their guests and we were all there at Vivien's invitation.

The spreading two-storey building is startlingly pink, pink as candy floss, its pinkness emphasised by the impossibly luscious green lawn and towering trees. An elegant colonnaded entrance leads into a world of status and privilege where reception is slick and professional, where voices are low. The staff are solemn, as if this is no place for frivolity, and in the soft afternoon sunshine, it did appear to be an establishment where decorum rules.

The parquet floor was polished to a mirror finish and squeaked as we walked through corridors wide enough to accommodate a Rolls Royce. A stuffed lion mounted on a wall in one of the hallways watched morosely as we followed our room steward – no tipping allowed – past walls decorated with cartoons depicting the antics of the famous and sometimes infamous members of long ago.

Our rooms looked just the way they were when I last stayed there more than fifty years ago. Spacious and comfortable but with no frills or furbelows and very much in the 1950s. The en-suite bathroom was similarly unchanged, its bathtub deep and large enough to accommodate a small rowing boat, with the original twiddly taps and window latches with the old-fashioned arms that have holes in. From our ground floor bedroom, we looked out onto pristine gardens where a lady was picking up the odd fallen leaf.

It is a quintessentially British establishment with an almost church-like atmosphere, no high-pitched squealing or hearty guffaws or children running around. It's a place where a gentleman may sit and read his newspaper with a tumbler of whisky at his elbow, or enjoy a game of chess. The décor is tastefully inviting, the oriental rugs are unwrinkled, the fireplace set with logs, the flowers in the vases are petal perfect and able to admire their reflections in the polished surfaces of the tables. A neatly folded Times newspaper, a chess board, standard lamps and potted palms give the lounge the air of a 1950s London gentleman's club. Service is smooth and professional – a raised finger brings a waiter swiftly.

Club rules are discreetly but strictly enforced. Any form of business or political discussion or meeting may only be conducted in the room specifically designed for that purpose. You can't walk around in the club with a briefcase, computer, tablet, file, notebook, mobile phone, camera or small child. Photography is not permitted within the club and photographs may not be shared to social media, which is why you will find very few photographs of the club in the public domain. I believe this rule was originally introduced to protect members who were keeping company with persons of the opposite sex with whom they should not have been keeping company.

You may not wear jeans, trainers, flip flops, t-shirts, shorts or skimpy tops, and talking is not permitted in the computer room. All purchases are signed for and settled by credit card. Cash does not change hands. Members and guests must dress appropriately for dinner.

It's quaint, and however I may feel about the British Empire and colonialists, there was something poignant at the thought of those early arrivals transplanted so far away from their families, friends and comfortable English homes into a strange and hostile land, facing innumerable difficulties and coming here to find some comfort and company.

After being pampered and cosseted for two weeks, free to dress as we wished and be completely relaxed in our surroundings, some of our group were puzzled and disconcerted by the restrictions in the club, and I suspected that only Vivien and I actually appreciated this place – probably the poshest club in Africa – because it is eccentrically British. It's a small island of Britishness, aesthetically old-fashioned, its charm lies in its history. It was pure nostalgia for me.

We met one of our group in the corridor, and he was shaking his head in bewilderment. Having heard so much about this club, this was not at all what he expected after the splendour of the places we had so far stayed in. Ageing sanitaryware and old-fashioned furnishings, why hadn't this place been updated? I tried to explain that this is not a hotel, it's an institution, but I think the subtlety was lost on him.

Discretion rules at Muthaiga. What happens there stays there. Generally. Which is why members could and can come here and behave as outrageously as they wish without fear of publicity. If they wished to ride their horses through the dining room, throw the furniture on the fire or shoot the glass out of the windows, that was fine as long as they paid for the damage. I don't know what goes on there now, but in its heyday it was known as a place of debauchery, where wives were swapped, ladies danced naked and the Prince of Wales was bombarded with bread rolls. The thing I loved about the club is its history, all those wild ghosts haunting its corridors. The Happy Valley set, the 'great white hunters', the dotty eccentrics, the privileged folk whose money and connections allowed them to behave outside the laws.

The last time I was here, I was eighteen, attending the Limuru Hunt Ball, regarded as one of the social events of the year. I remember the dress I wore. It was satin, in a deep shade of pink, fading from the scooped neck to paler pink at the waist and then gradually darkening down to the hem slightly above my knees, and stiletto heels in the same deep pink shade.

227

I was excited and nervous at the thought of spending an evening with the hunt servants, my first adult dance. My family did not move in the social circle that frequented the club, and regarded it with suspicion, as the lair of the lawless English upper classes and a den of dubious behaviour. How right they were. :) The elderly lady with whom I shared an office, raised an eyebrow when I told her I was going, and cautioned me – with a deeply meaningful look – to be very careful and to make sure I behaved myself.

It was such a glamorous affair, the men in DJs, the ladies in long dresses. I don't remember the meal, but that our table drank only champagne, the first I had ever tasted. And I can't remember at what point the mature guests dropped their best behaviour and started to let their hair down, but it certainly opened my eyes. Bread rolls flew from table to table, the waiters ducking as they delivered new courses. A champagne fight broke out, corks bounced off the walls, women shrieked, people swapped clothes, there were bawdy songs and we twisted the night away with Chubby Checker. No matter how much I drank, my glass was always full. The dance floor was slippery with champagne, the bow ties had come off, as had high heels, at least one frock and there were gentlemen's trousers draped over the backs of chairs.

At some point during the evening, a discussion arose regarding the perfect breast size and how it should fit into a champagne goblet with no space left, and no overflow. If at the beginning of the evening I had known that I would be stripping to the waist in a room full of people, I'd have turned tail and run away. But with the benefit of the torrent of champagne I had enjoyed, it seemed perfectly natural that the women at our table all bared their assets and tried, like Cinderella's sisters, to fit their womanly parts into the shallow glass, urged on by the men banging their cutlery noisily. As a six and a half stone, eighteen-year-old I had a distinct advantage and it really was no contest. When the sun came up, we ate bacon and eggs. Apart from the champagne goblet test, I think I behaved myself, but who knows? One of my shoes had vanished and was never seen again.

Vivien had arranged a farewell meal at the club, at which the guides would receive their bonuses. They had worked without a break for seventeen days, from before sunrise until after sundown. When we had washed after our visit to Ngando, and changed into our 'best' clothes, we sat down to lunch on the lawn at a table set with baskets of roses. All the team were there – Paul the taxi driver, Peter the student whose education Vivien has sponsored (who was hoping to go to the United States to continue his IT studies, with his ambition to work for Google), Herman, the company's CEO, together with his wife and daughters, Philemon from the office, along with all our fellow travellers and guides.

Kamara was seated to my right and I asked him if he was enjoying the meal, an elaborate chicken dish. He replied politely, 'yes, it was very good, but African food is better.' Then he added: 'Vivien took us all to Mount Kenya Safari Club and taught us how to eat properly, the way the English do, with a knife and fork,' looking pointedly across the table where some of our American friends were eating with just a fork, which is something I usually do. I quickly picked up my knife.

When the meal was finished, Dedan stood up to deliver a valedictory.

'Let me start by saying that the food was good – thank you very much. Send a message to the chef.'

He turned and smiled down the table.

'You are great people and without you we would not be here. Thank you very much. Let us thank God for the journey everywhere we have gone, and the journey is not yet over. You still have to fly, and we will be with you in prayers for everybody to go back to his or her destination safely, and when you get there we get an email or a message 'I am back home,' and we will say 'Allelujah, thanks be to God.'

'Thank you very much for everybody who made this safari, and I want to send my sincere thanks to Vivien. Vivien, you are great, you are wonderful, you are stupendous.' I chuckled because that's a word I had used the previous day and I knew he had stored it away.

'It is not easy to make this kind of a safari happen. It requires a lot of effort. We have been in this industry for quite some time, as Vivien has been for more than 26 years, and without the help of the office, it would not have been possible for us to organise this memorable safari. Mr Herman, thank you very much to your team.

'What I would request is that when you go back to your respective places, please be our ambassadors. Word of mouth is very, very important – that I was there myself, that I can introduce you to the person who organised the safari, and that is *As You Like It Safaris* under the leadership of Vivien Prince. We will be more than grateful.

'I am sure that there are a lot of people who have never visited Africa or Kenya. They think Kenya is Africa and Africa is Kenya. Showing your photographs that you took helps them to know exactly what you are talking about. Even if it's just one person, you have done your job. That person will pass your message to another person.

'Tell them that this is a hotbed of wildebeeste. Tell them that this is a hotbed of a beautiful Kilimanjaro view. Tell them that this is a hotbed of leopards with cubs in Samburu. In other words, help us to fight the negative information that is being passed out there by people who may never even visit Africa or Kenya.

'So thank you very much. And I also want to thank my fellow guides led by Mr Kamara. We had very good cooperation between us guides, and the expertise of each one of us I think helped us to be where we are, and this is a safari I think we will remember for years and years to come.'

Somebody called out good naturedly: 'Dedan, are you sure there are leopards in Samburu?' It was true that they had been elusive and the guides had had to work very hard and patiently to find them at all.

Dedan laughed. 'When you come back, I will not only show you a leopard being followed by its cub, but I will show you cubs nursing.

'Ladies and gentlemen, may God bless you. Those who have our contacts, we say, if I bid you goodbye it doesn't end there. It doesn't make us not see one another again. We also have an opportunity of seeing each other again in Heaven and we will all celebrate. Would that be good for you?

'So thank you very much, ladies and gentlemen. We at *As You Like It Safaris* believe that we are No. 1, but it is difficult to maintain to be No. 1 without your input. If there is anything that you were not happy about, you have Vivien's email, so tell her so that next time we know where we went wrong, and where we did well. We appreciate that you have paid a lot of money for this safari. We need you to get value for your money, and there is no excuse, there are no shortcuts. We must make sure that you get value for your money, and it is for you to let us know where we went wrong, how we can improve.

'Thank you very much, and I wish you the blessing of luck in all your undertakings, and I can see beautiful faces here, beautiful people.'

That was where our safari officially came to an end. Many of our group were already packed and ready to leave for the airport to catch evening flights. I was going to miss these people with whom we had spent the last fortnight.

Later, Terry and I took afternoon tea from a selection of dainty sandwiches and cakes, and tea served from a pot into bone china cups. It was an utterly English moment under the African sun, on the green lawn of Kenya's most exclusive club.

Neither of us was hungry in the evening, but we joined the remainder of our group who were dining at Pinks Brasserie, a more recent addition to the club where the dress rules and atmosphere are less formal. To be honest it did nothing for me; it just doesn't have the 'Muthaiga' charm. It's too modern and too casual and features my pet hate – a television in the restaurant. Sorry, Pinks. But for people who want a relaxed meal in beautiful surroundings, where children can run around, it's ideal. There was an end-of-term atmosphere among our friends who were all excited and ready to go home. I think I was the only person there who wished we could stay forever.

Conversation turned to how to deal with people who recline their seats on aircraft so that their heads are resting right in your lap. There were various suggestions ranging from using their heads to rest your book or magazine on, tapping them with a rolled-up newspaper, jerking them with your knees, or sneezing loudly next to their ears. I will not say who suggested what, because what is said in the club stays in the club.

Later in the evening, we ended up in the bar with Stacey and Mike, both animal lovers like ourselves. This was the first time we'd really had an opportunity to spend time any together. Stacey excused herself early, but by the time I tottered to bed, I'd drunk more Bailey's in one evening at Mike's insistence than I'd done previously in my entire life.

Chapter Thirty-one

SPEAK SWAHILI: RAFIKI – FRIEND

We were not leaving for another day, and to my surprise I woke up clear-headed when Vivien knocked on the door next morning, asking if we'd like to go with her to Elementeita, where she owned a plot of land. We had stopped there very briefly on our way back from the Masai Mara, and I'd asked her about an obelisk that I could see in the distance. She replied that it was the Cole memorial, but she didn't really know much about it. However, she knew a man who did, and she was going to introduce me to him.

We set off loaded with packed lunches supplied by the club so we could picnic at the farm. Our numbers had dwindled to dear Bob and Beth, Michael, Vivien, Kamara, Dedan and ourselves. Peter the young student came with us to surprise his father James, who lives at and looks after Vivien's land.

As we drove over the escarpment, Vivien decided to buy a kilo of carrots from a lady selling them at the roadside. Kamara was instructed to negotiate the price, and it took a few minutes to reach agreement as it appeared that like everything else, the more you bought, the cheaper the price, but you couldn't be told the price until you'd agreed on the quantity. As we moved off knee-deep in carrots, I remembered my first experience of Kenyan sales techniques.

When we first went to live in Kenya, it was a family tradition to go out for tea at the weekend to one of the many hotels or country clubs. One Sunday, we set off to Naivasha for tea at the Belle Inn. It was our first drive along this route, and the windows were wound down to allow cool air into the car. At the top of the escarpment, a crowd of small children stood in the road and my father had to stop the car to avoid running over them. Within seconds, the vehicle was full of wooden carvings, bundles of rhubarb and baby rabbits. Full! In the back seat, I could hardly see through a forest of rhubarb stalks and leaves. My father and mother were pushing things out through the front windows, and as fast as they went out they were swiftly pushed back in, while the children cried: '*Samuni! Samuni.*' A *samuni* was 50 cents, the equivalent of sixpence.

'Shut your windows!' my father shouted, but the *totos* were three deep, leaning in to the window space and my small arm was no match for their strength as I tried to wind my window up. The little people were on both sides and in front of the vehicle; we were caught in a *samuni* trap. My mother kept crying: 'Do something! Do something!' and I didn't know whether I was frightened or excited. My father took a handful of coins and flung them over the heads of the children, who turned and raced to gather them, allowing us a few seconds to unload most of the rhubarb and carvings. However, the baby rabbits had hidden themselves in small dark places, and we had to drive down the road to gather and release them. From then on, our windows always stayed firmly shut no matter how hot it was.

As we drove along towards Elementeita memories came trickling back. How many other times had I travelled on this road? Certainly many hundreds. To see the flamingos or watch motor racing at Nakuru. To visit a boyfriend who farmed at Gilgil; to visit friends at Thomson's Falls and Eldoret, for fishing trips to Lake Naivasha, this road had always been the highway to pleasure.

At Elementeita, we stopped at a long, low red brick bungalow surrounded by neat gardens of vivid shrubs and trees, overlooking the nearby lake. Now a hotel, a hundred years ago it was the home of one of the early aristocratic

British settlers, the splendidly named Galbraith Lowry Egerton Cole, second son of the Earl of Enniskillen. The obelisk that I had noticed earlier marks his burial place, and we had come here to learn more about him.

Joseph Kodonyo is a naturalist, ornithologist and an historian who was kind enough to offer to tell me the story of the ill-fated pioneer who had built and lived in this house.

If you had lived in Kenya then you would know the name Lord Delamere, who was the doyen of the pioneer settlers. In the 1950s, his statue dominated Delamere Avenue, the splendid tree-lined road that was Nairobi's main thoroughfare with its palm trees and lawns edged with prickly red, crown of thorns euphorbias. Delamere's statue is long gone, as the avenue was renamed after Jomo Kenyatta, but Delamere's name is written indelibly in the 20th century history of Kenya. When he married Galbraith Cole's sister, he gave his brother-in-law 30,000 acres of land which Cole called Kekopey, and on which he built his house.

On the wall in what was Cole's living room, is a gold-framed photograph of him. Below it reads an eulogistic inscription recording his death and that he is buried on the property. It's followed by a quote from Shakespeare's *Julius Caesar*: 'The elements so mixed in him that Nature might stand up and say to all the world: 'This was a man.'

The quote lacks the first few words, which are: 'His life was gentle'. It may or may not have been, but he was deported from Kenya for shooting dead a farm worker who had stolen one of his sheep, and his mother had to use her aristocratic influence for him to be allowed back into the country.

Joseph said that Elementeita was a sacred place for the Maasai, particularly the hot springs which were believed to have healing powers. When the first settlers arrived there, it was at a time when the Maasai and their herds had been weakened by drought and disease, and so they had entered into a consensual agreement in 1904, whereby the tribe would relocate to other areas and vacate the land leaving it for the people they called 'the White Cloud' for a period of one hundred years. In return, the settlers would offer them protection from other tribes and allow them access to fresh water at Naivasha as well as a safe corridor for the movement of their herds. Joseph continued that relations had been good between the tribe and Delamere, who was so popular with the Maasai who admired him, they had a saying: 'Be like Delamere'.

In 1911, the terms of the previous agreement were altered, and the Maasai found themselves moved and restricted to less-favourable areas.

When 2004 arrived, the original agreement would come to an end, and the 'White Cloud' would be expected to move on. But, of course, it didn't. It's still there and is at the root of unrest among the Maasai who would like their land back in accordance with the original agreement.

Getting back to Galbraith Cole – Joseph looked very sad. 'He was a very sick man, in great pain all the time, and he was blind in one eye. The pain was too much for him, and so he went to his favourite place and shot himself dead.' He pointed towards the obelisk. 'That is where he is buried.'

Cole was only 48 when he died. His brother Berkeley Cole, who was the founder of the Muthaiga Country Club, also died young from cardiac arrest, possibly due to his habit of drinking a bottle of champagne daily at mid-morning as Karen Blixen mentioned in *Out of Africa*. The Grim Reaper has no respect for the aristocracy.

The Cole family continued farming at Kekopey until the 1970s, when the estate was sold and divided into smallholdings. The main building with its parquet floors and stone fireplace still has the relaxed, nostalgic feel of an early settler's home, the bright and spacious rooms furnished for comfort and practicality more than effect. It is somewhere that, given the opportunity, I would love to stay and to accompany Joseph on his guided nature walks, because this place is not only historic but also absolutely teeming with spectacular bird life, and I cannot think of a better way to explore it other than with this wise and knowledgeable man.

Vivien's land is only a short drive away, just a couple of hundred yards from the lake, where we were greeted by two friendly dogs and a number of men – one of whom was wearing a trilby hat and a red, padded ski suit which looked somewhat out of place in the warm mid-day sunshine of the Rift Valley.

James was working as a groom when Vivien met him in 1992 at a racing stable where she rode. He and his wife later worked for her and had two children, Peter and his sister Muthoni. James was a strict father who guided his children towards being disciplined, focused and successful. Peter was a straight A student throughout his schooling and he was very ambitious; as I mentioned earlier, he wants to go to the United States and work for Google. Vivien and our fellow traveller Michael sponsored Peter at the American University in Nairobi, an outstanding school with the finest library in Africa, and one of the inspirational ways in which America has used her Third World Aid.

When Vivien bought her land it was entirely overgrown with prickly bushes, cactus, scrub and weeds until James volunteered to take care of and improve it. 'It is payback time,' he said. 'This is for my children's education.'

(Since our visit, Peter graduated in Software Engineering and is now progressing with his Master's Degree. His sister Muthoni followed in his footsteps, also sponsored by Michael and Vivien, and is studying sciences at the American University towards her ambition to become a doctor.) What a great example of how well-raised children from impoverished backgrounds can excel if they are given the chance.

Vivien waved her arm around. 'Look – James has cleared it all, by hand, without any machinery. He's the hardest working man I've ever known.'

Not only is he hard working, James is a very spiritual man who seems to have psychic abilities.

He told Vivien, 'I can do nothing without water. You must drill a borehole, right here,' and he pointed to a specific place on the land. Everyone insisted she would be wasting her money because lake Elementeita's water is saline, as is the water on all the neighbouring properties.

After the geologists had been and the necessary permits were obtained, they drilled. What they found was the largest flowing fresh water river imaginable, and no one could believe their eyes as the water gushed out.

We clustered around the borehole and when the pump was turned on, the water did indeed shoot out in a powerful fountain, cool and pure and sweet.

There were goats under and also up in the branches of acacia trees, birds everywhere, and a fenced area where a gang of African ladies were weeding and digging with hoes. James explained that they were preparing a patch where he was going to grow turf to cover the rest of the land where Vivien's house would be built.

As well as the two resident dogs, there were a couple of sleek puppies wriggling and running around. 'Where did these dogs come from?' she asked James.

He waved a hand vaguely and said, 'The woman who lives over there – she's gone to Nairobi for a few days and asked me to look after them.'

'Hmm,' said Vivien, 'I wonder. I know what he's like when it comes to dogs. He really loves them.'

I kept looking at the man wearing the ski suit. Was he perhaps suffering from some condition that meant the heat of Kenya's afternoon sun was insufficient to keep him warm? I didn't want to be rude but I just had to ask. He explained that it was like a suit of armour that he wore to protect himself from the sharp claws of the dogs who jumped up on the people they love. They loved him very much because he took them for walks down to the lake.

We spent a couple of peaceful hours wandering around in the sun, photographing the birds and collecting the lumps of glittering obsidian that littered the ground. In the absence of any furniture, we sat on upturned tree stumps and spread out the picnic on a rug on the ground. The ladies who were working on James's turf area were invited to join us, but they were very shy and uncomfortable in our company, preferring to take some food and go to eat it a distance away. I smiled to myself as I watched them piling their plates high with food from Muthaiga Country Club, their country's most exclusive establishment. I hoped they would enjoy it.

Chapter Thirty-two

SPEAK SWAHILI: KWAHERI – GOODBYE

Our time in Kenya had almost run out, and as we drove back to the club that afternoon I was watching every inch of the road, trying to soak up as many images as possible to take away with me. The wonky, optimistic shops and hotels; the straight-backed people in ragged clothes, the colourful pyramids of fruit and vegetables, the slogans on buses and lorries, the *boda bodas*, the goats and chickens.

That evening we retired early and began emptying our suitcases of all the things we no longer needed that could be useful for others – clothing, shoes and toiletries. Vivien had suggested we ladies brought panty liners in case we were ever in need of potty stops while out in the bush on drives. As I have a long-range tank, I'd had no need of them, and was about to put the unopened packets in the bin. 'Oh my goodness, no!' she shrieked. 'Haven't you any idea how precious these are to girls here? Most of them can't afford sanitary protection. These are such a luxury for them.' How little I still understood about life there.

We entered that limbo time zone when you are sitting around waiting to leave, half wanting time to stand still, the other half urging it to speed up, and then it was mid-afternoon and Kamara was waiting to drive us to the airport. I was determined not to cry, but my face was rigid as we climbed into the Land Cruiser for the last time. Just before we left, Dedan came over. 'You have forgotten something,' he said, handing me my hat. Oh Dedan, what are we going to do without you?

As we drove away, I began trying to use the power of my

mind to cause a breakdown, or a peaceful demonstration, or some kind of weather-related situation that would delay our flight and give us one more day.Alas, our drive was smooth and we arrived at the airport in good time. Kamara unloaded our luggage, and turned to say goodbye. Something that would have been almost unthinkable forty years ago was now entirely natural as we hugged.

While we waited to board the Swiss International plane, I was saying in my head: 'Still in Kenya. Still in Kenya.' The words went silently around and around, as we took our seats and buckled our belts, and as the plane began to taxi, and as it started its take-off run. 'Still in Kenya. Still in Kenya.' I kept repeating those words until the wheels clunked up and we were airborne.

Chapter Thirty-three

SPEAK SWAHILI: NDOTO NZURI
– SWEET DREAMS

Kenya is a country of such diversity.

Snowy mountains and silver-sanded beaches. Arid deserts and lush forests. Modern cities and age-old dwellings. Blazing heat and frosty mornings. The glare of the sun and the darkness of the night.

There is vast wealth and pitiful poverty. There are those who dream of riches and others who ask only for empty spaces and grazing for their cattle.

Everywhere you see people doing anything and everything they can to better themselves, or in some cases just to stay alive. They are so resilient, so optimistic, so humorous.

I am blessed to have been able to come back to remind myself how privileged and fortunate I was to have lived in this beautiful country.

One of my Kenyan friends, Simon Gisore, a good Samaritan and philanthropist, photographer and poet has perfectly captured what I feel.

The wind,
In it was a scent,
So hard to remember,
So hard to forget,
Memories long forgotten,
A past so vivid,

A stranger so familiar.

I wake up to a dream,
And see the wind,
In it is a scent,
So hard to remember,
So hard to forget,
Africa.
The scent of my childhood.

.

POSTSCRIPT

Head chef Fred Lemerle at the Little Mara Bush Camp did not fit the classic image of a Samburu. He was humble in appearance and a little shy, a hard-working man who wore chef's whites and was proud of his work and loved his job. We knew him only briefly, but he was certainly one of the people who stayed most clearly in our memory.

On the 4th of February 2016, he was returning from a visit to his family. He had a wife, two young children and a baby on the way. He posted on his Facebook page, asking for God's protection because he was a devout Christian:

'Thank you Lord, its another day I wake up and proceeding on another journey to Masai Mara. Please God grant mercies, it's a long journey.'

His next post read: 'Stuck in the bush, lots of rain.'

Fred never reached the camp. He was killed later that day in a road accident.

Lala salama, Fred.

Fred, Masai Mara 2015

MAP

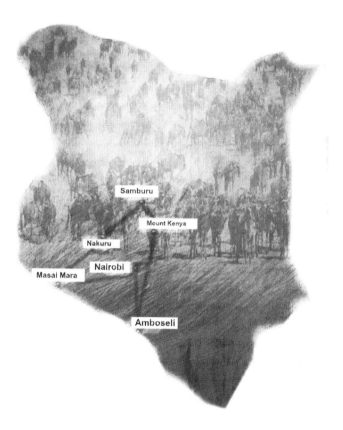

ACKNOWLEDGEMENTS

My thanks to Karrie Jacobs for her kind permission to quote from her article on Charles de Gaulle airport, published on http://www.travelandleisure.com

Special thanks to Simon Gisore for allowing me to quote his beautiful poem.

Thank you to all our fellow travellers for your friendship that added so much to our safari, and to our guides for all your hard work, humour and dedication.

Thank you to our proofreader Andrew Ives.

And thank you to Vivien who made it all happen.

Dear Reader,

Asante sana – thank you – for buying and reading *Safari Ants, Baggy Pants and Elephants*. I hope you enjoyed travelling with us around some of Kenya's wildlife reserves and meeting the people who made our trip so memorable. If you would like to continue the journey, please visit the Facebook page https://www.facebook.com/SafariAnts where I shall be regularly posting news and lovely photographs of Kenya, welcoming discussions and hoping to meet those of you who share my love for the country, or who would like to learn more about it. I look forward to talking with you.

   If you enjoyed travelling with me and could afford 5 minutes of your time to leave a review on Amazon.com (http://amzn.to/2pEGOMN) or Amazon.co.uk (http://amzn.to/2pTZ3im), I would be truly grateful. With more than 500,000 travel books on Amazon, it's hard for a new title to gain visibility, and if it's invisible nobody will find it. Authors depend on the goodwill and support of their readers to help them to grow their sales. Once a book has 25 reviews, Amazon will begin to give it a little boost on their sites. Once it has 50+ reviews, Amazon will actively start to promote it so that more readers can find it.

   By writing just a few words you can help make this book a success, and if you could do that for me, you will have my infinite gratitude. :)

Susie

This is the link to the on-line album and slide show of our safari: http://bit.ly/2rhZF1k

This is the link to join my (very infrequent!) mailing list: http://eepurl.com/zyBFP

(All email details securely managed at Mailchimp.com and never shared with third parties.)

LINKS

Hope Streams Academy
http://hopestreamsacademy.org/
Facebook:
https://www.facebook.com/HopeStreamsAcademy/

David Sheldrick Wildlife Trust Elephant Orphanage
https://www.sheldrickwildlifetrust.org/
Facebook: https://www.facebook.com/thedswt
Instagram: https://www.instagram.com/dswt/
Twitter: https://twitter.com/DSWT

AsyoulikeitSafaris
http://www.asyoulikeitsafaris.com/
Facebook: https://www.facebook.com/asyoulikeit.safaris/

The Masai Cricket Warriors
Facebook:
https://www.facebook.com/Maasai.Cricket.Warriors/

Susie Kelly
Safari slide show: http://bit.ly/2rhZF1k
Mailing list: http://eepurl.com/zyBFP
Facebook Safari Ants:
https://www.facebook.com/SafariAnts

MORE SUSIE KELLY TRAVEL BOOKS

I Wish I Could Say I Was Sorry
'*A Child Called It* meets *Out Of Africa* in this stunning
memoir of a woman's 1950s childhood in Kenya. Filled
with candid humor and insights, this authentic tale captures
one woman's incredible coming-of-age journey.' BookBub

*Swallows & Robins: The Laughs & Tears Of A Holiday
Home Owner*
Finalist, The People's Book Prize 2016
'Laugh out loud funny. A must-read for anyone dreaming
of the good life running gites in France.' *The Good Life
France*

*The Valley Of Heaven And Hell: Cycling In The Shadow of
Marie-Antoinette*
Novice cyclist Susie wobbles on her bike for 500 miles
through Paris and Versailles, the battlefields of World War
1, the Champagne region and more.

Travels With Tinkerbelle: 6,000 Miles Around France In A Mechanical Wreck
Join Susie, Terry and 2 huge dogs on a 6,000-mile journey around the perimeter of France.

Best Foot Forward: A 500-Mile Walk Through Hidden France
When Susie decides, at the age of 50+, on a whim, to trek alone across France from La Rochelle to Lake Geneva in Switzerland, she entrusts her French farmhouse full of assorted animals to a total stranger from San Antonio, Texas. *Audiobook Also Available*

The Lazy Cook (1) Quick & Easy Meatless Meals
The first of Susie's delightful round-ups of her favourite quick, simple, easy recipes, sprinkled with anecdote and humour.

The Lazy Cook (2) Quick & Easy Sweet Treats
'I like a dessert to make me feel slightly guilty about eating it, but not enough to make me stop.'

Two Steps Backward (Bantam)
The trials and tribulations of moving a family and many animals from the UK to a run-down smallholding in SW France. *Paperback only, UK only.*

Blackbird Digital Books
The #authorpower publishing company
Discovering outstanding authors
www.blackbird-books.com
@Blackbird_Bks

Blackbird

·

16554376R00161

Made in the USA
San Bernardino, CA
17 December 2018